Redeeming Promises
Lenten Devotions

Brooke Holt

Redeeming Promises
Lenten Devotions

© Brooke Holt. All rights reserved.

Published in Jacksonville, FL by Bible Study Media, Inc.

ISBN # 978-1942243-68-7

No part of this publication may be reproduced, stored in a retrieval system, or transmitted in any form or by any means electronic, mechanical, photocopy, recording, or otherwise, except for brief quotations in printed reviews without the prior written permission of the publisher. www.biblestudymedia.com

Unless otherwise indicated, all Scripture quotations are from the ESV® Bible (The Holy Bible, English Standard Version®, copyright © 2001 by Crossway, a publishing ministry of Good News Publishers. Used by permission. All rights reserved.

Printed in the United States of America.

An Invitation to a Holy Lent

Dear People of God:

The first Christians observed with great devotion the days of our Lord's passion and resurrection, and it became the custom of the Church to prepare for them by a season of penitence and fasting. This season of Lent provided a time in which converts to the faith were prepared for Holy Baptism. It was also a time when those who, because of notorious sins, had been separated from the body of the faithful were reconciled by penitence and forgiveness, and restored to the fellowship of the Church. Thereby, the whole congregation was put in mind of the message of pardon and absolution set forth in the Gospel of our Savior, and of the need which all Christians continually have to renew their repentance and faith. I invite you, therefore, in the name of the Church, to the observance of a holy Lent, by self-examination and repentance; by prayer, fasting, and self-denial; and by reading and meditating on God's holy Word. And, to make a right beginning of repentance, and as a mark of our mortal nature, let us now kneel before the Lord, our maker and redeemer.

(From the Book of Common Prayer Ash Wednesday Service)

How to Be Reconciled to God
Ash Wednesday

"Therefore, we are ambassadors for Christ, God making his appeal through us. We implore you on behalf of Christ, be reconciled to God. For our sake he made him to be sin who knew no sin, so that in him we might become the righteousness of God." 2 Corinthians 5:20-21

Today is a high and holy day in the life of the church – Ash Wednesday – and it is the invitation to be reconciled to God. Yes, every day is an invitation to be reconciled to God, but the church sets this day apart as a day for fasting. Many Christians go to church and receive the sign of the cross marked with ashes upon their forehead while they hear these words: *"Remember that you are dust, and to dust you shall return"* (Genesis 3:19, cited in the Book of Common Prayer, Ash Wednesday, p. 265).

Why would someone choose to fast when we have such an abundance of food available to us? Fasting is an opportunity to deny the desires of the flesh so that one may be more attentive to the way of the Spirit. No, it is not fun, but removing some of the earthly comforts you enjoy allows you to recognize ways in which you choose comfort over holiness (sin instead of obedience). This time of denial is designed to create a hunger within you not for the things of the world but for the things of the Lord – the fruit of the Spirit, justice, love, holiness, healing, etc.

Paul writes to the church in Corinth to remind them and you that Jesus denied the desires of his flesh all the way to the cross. There, he took on your sin so that you could then receive his righteousness – a holy exchange! If Jesus, the perfect Son of God, was willing to suffer death on a cross for you, are you willing to give up those earthly things that distract you from him?

I don't know what those things are for you, but you do. Scrolling through Facebook can replace your time of reading the Bible; Sunday Pickleball or golf can replace your time of worship; a belly that is always full can allow you to forget the starving people throughout the world or right around the corner from your workplace.

What would it look like for you to fast from those things for the next 40 days that you might be reconciled to Christ and to the body of Christ? That is the call of Ash Wednesday and the season of Lent – to allow the Holy Spirit to search you, to know you, and to convict you of the ways in which you are satisfying your fleshly appetites and missing the heart of God.

Will you take this season to be searched, known, and convicted? Jesus paid the price for your every sin and offers you his righteousness. May this Lenten season be one in which you grow daily in righteousness as you release the things of this world.

Reflection:

How is God calling you to fast today and throughout this Lenten season?

Living in the Steadfast Love of the Lord
Thursday

"The LORD is merciful and gracious, slow to anger and abounding in steadfast love. He will not always chide, nor will he keep his anger forever. He does not deal with us according to our sins, nor repay us according to our iniquities." Psalm 103:8-10

Growing up, I often said these infamous words to my parents: "That is not fair!" As the firstborn of four girls, I was very concerned with what seemed fair and right. My parents seemed to have a higher standard for me, which often perplexed and frustrated me. I can remember my mom repeatedly responding to me with that familiar phrase: "Life is not fair."

Now that I have three grown children of my own, I understand my parents were right. Life is not fair, and I appreciate that God is not fair either. He never has been, has he? Instead of being fair, God has been merciful and gracious to his people. He has been patient, and his love has not failed despite the disbelief and rebellion of his people.

When the Israelites found themselves as slaves in the land of Egypt, the Lord heard their cries, and he rescued them. Miraculously, the Lord worked on behalf of Israel: through Moses as their leader, plagues, parting the Red Sea, leading his people by a pillar of cloud each day and a cloud of fire at night (Exodus 13). God manifested his mercy, grace, patience, and steadfast love through this redemptive work and provision.

Long after Moses and the stubborn Israelites, the Lord sent his Son for the greatest rescue mission ever. Though his children had hard hearts and ignorant minds, Jesus dwelt among them. Jesus taught, healed, and eventually gave up his very life that those who would believe in him would have forgiveness of sin and everlasting life. It is not fair that a perfect man died on behalf sin, yet it is the greatest gift ever given!

As we begin the season of Lent, David's words in Psalm 103 serve to remind you that though you sin and fall short of the glory of God (everyone does), God sees beyond that sin and failure. Because of his great mercy, grace, patience, and steadfast love, the Lord sees the blood of Christ covering that sin – that is certainly not fair but so very good!

Reflection:

Ponder how God has poured out his mercy, grace, and steadfast love into your life. How have you responded to his faithfulness?

Are You Living in Freedom or Shame?
Friday

"For as high as the heavens are above the earth, so great is his steadfast love toward those who fear him; as far as the east is from the west, so far does he remove our transgressions from us. As a father shows compassion to his children, so the LORD shows compassion to those who fear him. For he knows our frame; he remembers that we are dust." Psalm 103:11-14

Jesus died that you may be free – free from the penalty of sin, the fear of death, and bondage to the evil forces of this world. Satan cannot steal your freedom. However, he can steal your joy. Though your sins are forgiven through Jesus' blood shed on the cross, many believers are held captive by the grips of shame. That shame is the ongoing message you hear of condemnation for your sins and mistakes, ongoing regret, a desire to pay the price, the need to be better, do better, etc. Sadly, shame is quite prevalent in the church today.

If Jesus paid such a high price for his followers to live in freedom, why does shame still hold so many professing believers captive? Think for a moment – does shame hold you or control you in any way? Are you truly living in the freedom that Jesus came to give you?

If you are struggling with shame, read the passage of Scripture for today again. The love of the Lord for you is steadfast meaning it is complete. It is so great that you cannot comprehend it.
And though you sin and will continue to sin, the Lord does not hold those transgressions against you. Instead, he sees you as separate from those transgressions; they are removed *"as far as the east is from the west"* (Psalm 103:12). Isn't that just amazing? When the Lord looks at you, he does not see sin but righteousness, the righteousness of his Son. That is who you are to him —
the righteousness of Jesus.

If that is how the Lord sees you, can you learn to see yourself through his eyes of grace, mercy, and forgiveness? The psalm goes on to explain that as your maker, the Lord fully understands your frame – *"he remembers that you are dust"* (Psalm 103:14). Those words are to be liberating to your soul. God understands why you can't live perfectly, and he sent his Son to do that for you.

Are you ready to live free from shame? Are you ready to receive the abundant forgiveness of the Lord? Today is the day to confess your unbelief, the ways you have remained in shame, to let those things go, and then receive the freedom that Jesus has for you.

Reflection:

How can you use this Lenten season to let go of shame by receiving the forgiveness of the Lord?

Are You Walking in the Ways of God or Man?
Saturday

"Beware of practicing your righteousness before other people in order to be seen by them, for then you will have no reward from your Father who is in heaven." Matthew 6:1

Whose affirmation have you sought to gain throughout your life? Is it from your mother, father, teachers, coaches, or friends? Seeking affirmation is not wrong; it is the way in which you seek affirmation that leads you astray. As God's beloved child, he would have you seek his approval above all else. This season of Lent is a wonderful opportunity to reorient the ways in which you seek affirmation and approval in this life.

In the early church, the season of Lent served as a forty-day period to prepare the candidates for baptism. The early church used the same practices we heard in church on Ash Wednesday: self-examination, repentance, prayer, fasting, self-denial, reading, and meditating on God's Word. These good spiritual practices are designed to lead one closer to the Lord and deeper in the ways of the Spirit.

Surely, the Lord loves the spiritual practices of his church, right? Just as the nation of Israel was often reprimanded for going through the motions – praying, fasting, and bringing sacrifices before the Lord, so would the Lord challenge you today. What is your Lenten spiritual discipline and why are you doing it? Are you seeking the affirmation of people or the affirmation of the Lord? Does your discipline lead you to godly humility or spiritual pride? Does your spiritual discipline glorify God or yourself?

We ask ourselves these important questions as the Lord has never delighted in his people going through the motions of religion. Instead, the Father looks for those who love him, seek to know him, glorify him, and to be transformed into the image of his Son. You have a choice here in this first week of Lent. You can seek the rewards of people or the rewards of the Father. What matters is the posture of your heart.

As you begin this holy season of Lent, ask the Lord to search your heart and to reveal your sinful desires and tendencies. Ask him to reveal the ways in which you still operate in the flesh instead of the Spirit, then ask for the Holy Spirit to empower you to choose his ways.

May this season be one in which you seek to truly grow in knowledge, love, and obedience to the Lord. That is what delights the heart of your Father and brings glory to his name here on earth. Practice these godly disciplines not for man but for the Father who will reward from heaven.

Reflection:

What is your Lenten spiritual discipline? Bring that before the Lord seeking his plans for you and his work in you.

Week of the First Sunday in Lent

Mighty to Save
Sunday

"Almighty God, whose blessed Son was led by the Spirit to be tempted by Satan: Come quickly to help us who are assaulted by many temptations; and, as you know the weaknesses of each of us, let each one find you mighty to save; through Jesus Christ your Son our Lord, who lives and reigns with you and the Holy Spirit, one God, now and for ever. Amen."

The Collect for the First Sunday in Lent, BCP

A great desire within every human heart is to be understood. The Collect for this week reflects that human desire. The prayer is that the Lord would not only see us and understand us but then that he would come to our rescue. In this season of Lent, we need the assurance of the Lord's understanding as well as his power to save. How can a perfect God understand man's weakness and inclination to sin? God understands because he hasn't just watched his people; he has lived among them and has experienced the temptations and the weaknesses of humanity.

After his baptism, Jesus was driven into the desert, where he endured a period of fasting and intense temptation by Satan. In his humanity, Jesus felt the hunger, the thirst, and the propensity towards fulfilling fleshly desires (by turning stones into loaves of bread). When Satan tempted Jesus to throw himself off the mountain, it was a lure toward human pride. How exciting it would be for the crowds to see angels appearing to catch Jesus as he fell. Jesus could demonstrate to the world who he was and how important he was to the Father.

Finally, the last and greatest temptation came when Satan took Jesus up the mountain, showed him all the kingdoms, and then promised Jesus all the glory without the pain. Satan would give Jesus all these kingdoms and all their glory if Jesus would just bow down and worship him. No rejection. No road to Calvary.

No cross.

Through each temptation, Jesus quoted Scripture back to Satan and surrendered to the plan of the Father and the timing of the Father. Jesus would receive perfect nourishment from the angels after the forty days.

At the death of Jesus, the Lord worked many physical phenomena – the curtain of the temple was torn in two, the earth shook, rocks were split, tombs were opened, and those who had been dead were raised and appeared to many; then there was a great earthquake (Matthew 27:51-54).

Creation displayed the atrocities of that day. After these events and his subsequent death and resurrection, Jesus sat at the right hand of the Father, and when he returns to the earth as the true king, every knee will bow, and every tongue will confess that Jesus Christ is Lord.

Jesus knew temptation, and Jesus knew how to overcome that temptation. Thus, Jesus fully understands your temptations; he understands your weaknesses and longs to help you to overcome these temptations. The writer of Hebrews attested to this truth: *"For because he himself has suffered when tempted, he is able to help those who are being tempted"* (Hebrews 2:18). Jesus stands ready to help you, not to condemn you.

Many Christians experience shame in their weaknesses, sinful actions, and thoughts. That shame has led them to hide from the Lord. Hiding leads to further sinning, whereas admitting and crying out for help leads to freedom. How do you approach the Lord with your own sin and weakness? Do you also run and hide, or do you walk into the light and allow the Lord to meet you in your weakness, to cover you with his mercy and grace, and then empower you by his Holy Spirit?

Satan is the father of condemnation, whereas God is the Father of compassion, mercy, and grace. Paul wrote about this amazing grace to the church in Corinth:

"But he said to me, 'My grace is sufficient for you, for my power is made perfect in weakness.' Therefore I will boast all the more gladly of my weaknesses, so that the power of Christ may rest upon me. For the sake of Christ, then, I am content with weaknesses, insults, hardships, persecutions, and calamities. For when I am weak, then I am strong" (2 Corinthians 12:9-10).

These words are meant to be liberating. Not only are you understood, but there is hope and help in your time of need.

What if your Lenten discipline this year was to acknowledge your weaknesses so that you could experience the strength of the Lord? The Lord knows that you are but dust; the Lord understands your weaknesses and your failures; and the Lord chooses to lavish you with his steadfast love and grace. May you truly find him mighty to save this Lenten season!

Reflection:

Where do you look in times of temptation and trial? How could you allow the Lord to be strong in your weakness?

Divine Affirmation
Monday

"In those days Jesus came from Nazareth of Galilee and was baptized by John in the Jordan. And when he came up out of the water, immediately he saw the heavens being torn open and the Spirit descending on him like a dove. And a voice came from heaven, 'You are my beloved Son; with you I am well pleased.'" Mark 1:9-11

Children grow up and desperately seek their parents' affirmation and approval…until their teenage years. Then, they secretly crave it while behaving in many contrary ways. Athletes seek the affirmation of their coaches, and students long for the approval of their teachers. We love affirmation! We love affirmation because we are glory magnets. Remember, we are made in the image of the triune God. In him is the fullness of glory. If God is all-glorious, then everything that he does reflects that glory. As people made in his image, we are created also to reflect glory. The problem is that our glory magnets get broken through the years. We forget that the source of our glory is God; it is not our works, our approval ratings, or even our righteousness. The result is that we seek our own glory. We perform, strive, compete, and always seek to prove our value and worth. It is an exhausting quest for glory that never completely fulfills us.

Thankfully, in the life of Jesus Christ, we learn a different way, a better way. On the day when Jesus was baptized, he had not done any ministry. The glory of Jesus was that though he was fully human, he was also fully divine. In his divinity, Jesus experienced all the temptations of human nature but remained without sin. Despite his sinless record, Jesus chose to identify with the sin of mankind. Requesting to be baptized by John demonstrated his identification with the nation of Israel and with us.

Though perfect, Jesus went under the waters of baptism for repentance to fulfill all righteousness. As he rose out of the waters, something unthinkable occurred.

The heavens were torn open, and the Spirit descended like a dove upon him. To explain this remarkable occurrence, a voice came from heaven with the words we all long to hear: *"You are my beloved Son; with you, I am well pleased"* (verse 11). Before Jesus had done anything on behalf of the Father and the kingdom of God, he was loved by the Father. The Father not only loved him but was pleased with him.

What we see in Jesus is the perfect Son but also the mystery of God's love. His love for Jesus was not based on Jesus' good works, the miracles he performed, or his great preaching and teaching. God's love for Jesus was because he was his Son. As the Son and as part of the Trinity, Jesus belonged to the Father. He was family.

In Jesus, we are made part of God's family. When we undergo the waters of baptism, all our sin is washed away; we have a clean slate. Instead of sin, we are covered in the righteousness of Jesus Christ. It is given to us just as if we had lived a perfect life. Jesus did what we could not do so that we could enjoy a relationship with the Father. And not just any relationship – we are his sons and his daughters. He is pleased when he looks upon us, seeing us through his Son.

Lent is a season in which we are to turn from our sins and turn whole-heartedly back to the Lord. It is also a season in which we are called to marvel at the righteousness that has been given to us through Jesus Christ. Jesus, too, was called to deny himself, to pick up his cross, and to surrender to the will of the Father. Because of his perfect obedience, we have the gift of salvation, eternal life, and forgiveness of our sins. We are called to live as people who have been washed clean and want to remain clean so that the glory of the Father can be reflected in our lives.

Our identity is found in being called the children of God – his beloved children and the children in whom he is well pleased. This Lenten season, may we embrace this identity and all the affirmation that comes with it! There is no reason to perform, to strive, or to compete. We have perfect righteousness and the promise of glory through the Son!

Reflection:

How are you seeking affirmation in this world? What would it look like to surrender your seeking and start resting in what has been done for you? You are already loved, delighted in, and fully affirmed in the eyes of your heavenly Father.

Desert Trials
Tuesday

"The Spirit immediately drove him out into the wilderness. And he was in the wilderness forty days, being tempted by Satan. And he was with the wild animals, and the angels were ministering to him." Mark 1:12-13

Jesus, John the Baptist, and all those present at the Jordan River during Jesus' baptism witnessed a miracle. The excitement must have been overwhelming for them. Until John the Baptist, the nation of Israel had not had a prophet for four hundred years. With John came the call to a baptism of repentance for the forgiveness of sins and the proclamation that the kingdom of heaven was at hand. The days of Israel's waiting were finally coming to an end. Hope was here!

Hope must have escalated as the heavens tore open, the Spirit descended like a dove, and a voice came down from heaven. Jesus was the very Son of God, the promised Messiah. Expectations for a new kingdom were high. The Jewish people could be free from the oppressive rule of the Romans. Finally, they could take their rightful place in the world as God's chosen people. The way ahead looked so bright!

Unfortunately, the way ahead did not look the way many anticipated. Using one of Mark's favorite words, "The Spirit immediately drove [Jesus] out into the wilderness" (v. 12). Jesus had no time to revel in the glory of his baptism; instead, he was driven into the discomfort of the wilderness where he spent forty days and forty nights fasting. After those forty days, Satan came to him with an arsenal of temptations.

Notice that when Jesus was baptized, he was already without sin. He had done nothing wrong, yet he still was led into this place of discomfort and testing. We may think that our painful places or our times of temptation are the result of our sin; however, they are often not related to our works but to the works of our enemy.

Just as Jesus continually faced the enemy and all his spiritual forces, so we will face that same enemy and those spiritual forces. In the Gospel of John, Jesus referred to Satan as the thief: *"The thief comes only to steal and kill and destroy. I came that they may have life and have it abundantly"* (John 10:10). This thief does not know us as the Lord knows us; however, he knows our general weakness and our susceptibility to things like hunger, fatigue, grief, and fear, and he is not afraid to attack us while we are down.

On the flip side, he is not afraid to attack while we are up, either. People warn about our mountaintop experiences and how glorious and uplifting they are until we return home, where all the temptations, habits, and systems are waiting to strip us of that glory and joy. Where Jesus came to give us abundant life, the thief came to strip us of that abundant life, to destroy.

Jesus was driven into the desert. As we begin the Lenten season, we are ushered into a time of self-denial, confession, and repentance. It is a somber season that precedes the great victory we celebrate on Easter day. Before the celebration comes the humiliation of the cross. Humility precedes glory. That is the invitation of Lent: humility before the Lord. It is the time in which we throw off all our pretenses and excuses. Without those coverings, we can see our sins clearly. We don't see our sin so that we can remain in it; we see it to turn from it, repent of it, and choose God's way.

The season of Lent is not a punishment for our wrongdoings. It is not a time in which the Lord wants us to feel guilt and condemnation; those are tools of the thief, not Jesus. Lent is a time of reflection, self-assessment, self-denial, and surrender to the Lord. At the end of Lent is the glorious celebration of Easter. It is a celebration well worth the forty days of challenge.

Reflection:

How do you view these forty days of Lent? Do you see the opportunity to truly know yourself so that you can return wholeheartedly to the Lord?

Not Everything Is What It Seems
Wednesday

"For Christ also suffered once for sins, the righteous for the unrighteous, that he might bring us to God, being put to death in the flesh but made alive in the spirit." 1 Peter 3:18

Many of us know the quote: "Not everything is what it seems" (Jose Saramago). The Apostle Peter probably had not heard that exact quote since Mr. Saramago lived many years after him. However, Peter was trying to encourage his reader with similar words – sometimes it looks like evil is winning, but God is always behind the scenes, working things according to his plan and purpose. The churches to whom Peter wrote were experiencing extreme abuse and persecution by the religious and civil authorities. If Jesus had overcome the world, why did evil seem to be winning?

The greatest example of things not being what they seemed was the crucifixion of Jesus Christ. While evil rallied all its forces together, God never lost control. When Jesus was betrayed, condemned, and crucified, the Lord never left his throne. He never threw up his hands in the air with confusion. The Lord knew the plan. It was not an easy plan, but it was the way of salvation. Jesus, the spotless lamb of God, took the sin of the world upon himself. The wrath of God towards sin came upon the one righteous man. While it seemed unfair and unjust, the Lord's justice was being satisfied. Through the blood of Jesus, all of humankind was invited into a relationship with the Father. They were offered forgiveness of sin, salvation, and reconciliation with the Lord. What appeared to be death instead brought life, and not just life for one but life for all who would put their trust in him.

Throughout the Lenten season, it can appear or feel like we are losing. The battle with sin rages as we seek to deny our fleshly desires. The pain of our sin becomes clear as we acknowledge all the ways in which we have fallen short of the glory of God. Forty days can begin to feel like forty years.

However, the cross is before us, and yet the cross is behind us. We already have the gift of salvation; we already have the gifts of forgiveness and reconciliation. The opportunity of Lent is to grow deeper into that salvation and deeper into the righteousness of Christ. In doing so, we go deeper into who we are made to be and called to be. Viewed properly, it is a glorious opportunity, though not always pleasant or pain-free.

The Lord would use this season of Lent to allow you to die to your flesh so that you may live in the fullness of his Spirit. It may not be easy, but there will be a great celebration at the end. In the meantime, things are not what they seem. The struggle between the flesh and the Spirit remains, but the true battle has already been won through the death and resurrection of Jesus Christ.

Reflection:

Do you become easily discouraged in challenging seasons? How would the Lord like to strengthen you in body, mind, and Spirit through this season of Lent?

To You, O Lord, I Lift Up My Soul
Thursday

"To you, O Lord, I lift up my soul. O my God, in you I trust; let me not be put to shame; let not my enemies exult over me. Indeed, none who wait for you shall be put to shame; they shall be ashamed who are wantonly treacherous." **Psalm 25:1-3**

Appropriate to the first Sunday in Lent, Psalm 25 is a lament. While there are expressions of faith in the Lord's mercy, there are also confessions of sin and acknowledgments of our need for salvation. To fully appreciate the words of Psalm 25, it is good to look back to Psalm 24, in which David asked the question: *"Who shall ascend the hill of the Lord? And who shall stand in his holy place?"* (Psalm 24:3). In essence, David was asking who are those who truly seek the Lord, and who can enter the worship of a holy God? David answered his own question: *"He who has clean hands and a pure heart"* (Psalm 24:4). To have clean hands and a pure heart would be to faithfully uphold the first two commandments of the Lord – to worship God alone and to make no idols. Exclusive worship of the Lord was required.

At the beginning of this Psalm, David proclaims his dedication to the Lord by stating that he will bow down to Him alone. By lifting up his soul, David expresses his whole-hearted devotion to God. As the king of Israel, David strives to lead his people towards a committed relationship with the Lord. Trusting in God alone, rather than forming alliances with the neighboring nations, would distinguish King David and the people of Israel from other nations. These nations often relied on one another for assurance, protection, and security, while Israel relied solely on God.

With this declaration of trust came David's plea to the Lord to be faithful to them, to protect them, and to display his glory to those who would oppose Israel. David's and Israel's hope were firmly grounded in God alone.

David declared that hope and then reminded God to acknowledge their faithfulness and to remain faithful to Israel in turn. It's as if he were reminding God, but likely he was reminding himself; David said that none who waited on the Lord would be put to shame. Instead, those who opposed the Lord were the objects of shame. Unlike Israel, these people and nations would eventually see and experience the futility of their misguided hope and trust.

As we begin the season of Lent, we are called to renew our commitment to the Lord and repent for seeking security, protection, and hope in this world. Just before receiving ashes on our foreheads, the priest prays: "Almighty God, you have created us out of the dust of the earth: Grant that these ashes may be a sign of our mortality and penance, so that we may remember that it is only through your gracious gift that we are given eternal life; through Jesus Christ our Savior. Amen" (Ash Wednesday service, p. 265 BCP). We are mere mortals, here for only a short time, while God is the immortal one, whose promises never fail. God offers eternal life through his Son, and we can receive forgiveness of sins and reconciliation by turning to him.

May we embrace David's confidence during this Lenten season. God remains faithful to his people. Shall we lift up our hearts in worship to this trustworthy God, acknowledging our sins and failures while placing our full trust in the work of Jesus Christ on our behalf?

Reflection:

To whom or what do you lift up your heart? In whom or what do you put your trust? How is the Lord calling you to a renewed commitment to him this Lenten season? That renewal begins with the acknowledgment that you have looked to other people and other things, followed by repentance. We can acknowledge our sin and turn from it because of the great salvation given to us in Christ Jesus. Repent but do not despair! Through Jesus, we have hope.

Godly Focus and Intention
Friday

"Make me to know your ways, O Lord; teach me your paths. Lead me in your truth and teach me, for you are the God of my salvation; for you I wait all the day long." Psalm 25:4-5

We are quite easily distracted in this world; at least, I am. We see a vision or feel a strong calling of the Lord to change our ways, to begin something new, to step out in faith; then, something or someone needs our attention. New bills to pay or unexpected challenges arise, and we forget. We forget the conviction, the vision, and the calling. As we heard in the service on Ash Wednesday, "Remember that you are dust, and to dust you shall return" (BCP, p. 265). We are frail people who forget who we are, whose we are, and what we are meant to do during our time here on earth.

Even though he was a great leader, King David (author of Psalm 25) must have struggled with these same issues. Knowing himself, David asked the Lord to make his ways known, to teach David how to faithfully walk on his paths, and to guide David into his truth. King David longed for God to provide his divine guidance for him and for the nation of Israel. God's ways were the best ways; King David trusted that the Lord would guide him and that nation of Israel into blessing and abundant life within the land he had given to them.

To know God's ways requires that one know God. When David prayed for the Lord to make him know his ways, David was asking that God reveal himself and his plans. Thankfully, the Lord had revealed himself through the teachings and writings of Moses and the prophets. The ways of God are to love him, to love one another, to show mercy, to love justice, and to seek faithfulness. God's way is the way of obedience.

God's paths are also lined with obedience and obedient action. It is one thing to know God and to know his revealed plans; it is another thing to act on that truth and guidance of the Lord. David wanted to know God's ways, to know God's paths so that he could do what God was calling him to do. There was the mental assent to God's ways and truth that must be followed by an obedient follow-through on those ways.

When David asked that God lead him in his truth and to continue to teach him, he longed for God's Word to dwell richly in his heart, to be the center of who he was, and to be the foundation for how he lived his life. Again, there was a full acknowledgement that God's ways were good and right, trustworthy, and true; they were worthy of David's full submission and adherence. David knew that salvation was found in none other than the Lord and that though he may have to wait, God would lead him in this way of faithfulness.

In this first week of Lent, it is the opportune time to make David's prayer your prayer. It is the time to ask the Lord to search your life and to reveal the ways that you have forgotten him, forgotten his convictions, forgotten what he has called you to do. Then it is time to recommit your heart, mind, and life to him, to seek the Lord and to fully surrender to his ways, his paths, and his truths.

Reflection:

Do you struggle with whole-heartedly trusting in God's ways, paths, and truth? If so, can you spend some time asking the Lord to create in you this faith of David?

The Steadfast Love of the Lord
Saturday

"Remember your mercy, O Lord, and your steadfast love, for they have been from of old. Remember not the sins of my youth or my transgressions; according to your steadfast love remember me, for the sake of your goodness, O Lord!" **Psalm 25:6-7**

Yesterday, we read King David's request for God to reveal his ways, his paths, and his truth. David desired for those ways of God, those truths of God to be ingrained within his very being so that he could faithfully walk with God and lead God's people. Today, David remembered God's revelation to Moses:

"The Lord descended in the cloud and stood with him there, and proclaimed the name of the Lord. The Lord passed before him and proclaimed, 'The Lord, the Lord, a God merciful and gracious, slow to anger, and abounding in steadfast love and faithfulness, keeping steadfast love for thousands, forgiving iniquity and transgression and sin'" (Exodus 34:5-7).

The Lord could not reveal his full glory to Moses, so he revealed these attributes of his glory: mercy, graciousness, patience, steadfast love, faithfulness, and forgiveness.

This self-revelation of God to Moses was to encourage him to remain faithful in leading a wayward people. While the Lord was perfectly holy, he understood the frailty of his creation. Instead of executing justice against their sin, God showed mercy time and time again.

King David put his trust in this mercy, grace, and steadfast love of the Lord. He knew that God saw all his shortcomings and all his sin, yet in seeing David's fallen state, God chose to show him mercy. It was mercy grounded and anchored in the steadfast love of God for his people. David trusted in this mercy of the Lord because he experienced it so profoundly.

While King David did great things for the Lord, David also sinned greatly before the Lord in his adulterous acts with Bathsheba and then in having her husband killed. With just these two acts, the king of Israel broke four of the Ten Commandments: You shall not commit adultery; you shall not murder; you shall not steal; and you shall not covet your neighbor's house, wife, servant, ox, or donkey (Exodus 20:3-17). David didn't just make a mistake, David made royal mistakes! As we know, the cost was great to David as well as to Bathsheba, but God's redemption of David's mistakes was even greater.

David had personally experienced the mercy of the Lord coupled with his steadfast love. Those experiences taught David the importance of obedience as well as the grace that held him when he failed. Lent is our invitation to experience these divine gifts. As Paul wrote to the Roman church, *"for all have sinned and fall short of the glory of God"* (Romans 3:23), but the story doesn't end there. In his mercy, grace, patience, and steadfast love, God provided for our salvation and forgiveness. The love of the Lord is perfectly secure. For those who put their trust in the salvific work of his Son, there is no way to out-sin his grace.

The invitation of the Lenten season is to look into a mirror and to see our sin and to confess that sin to the Lord while trusting in his mercy, grace, and steadfast love. We lament what we have done and all the ways we have fallen short while we trust that God's grace is working something glorious in us. We are never to stay comfortable in sin, but to turn and to seek to walk faithfully with the Lord.

Reflection:

Take time today to thank the Lord for his mercy, grace, and steadfast love. Soak in those glorious attributes of the Lord. He has you and he will never let you go. In that place of security, confess your sin and allow God's grace to wash you clean.

Week of the Second Sunday in Lent

God's Abundant Mercy
Sunday

"O God, whose glory it is always to have mercy: Be gracious to all who have gone astray from your ways, and bring them again with penitent hearts and steadfast faith to embrace and hold fast the unchangeable truth of your Word, Jesus Christ your Son; who with you and the Holy Spirit lives and reigns, one God, for ever and ever. Amen."

The Collect for the Second Sunday in Lent, BCP

The Lenten call to self-examination, self-denial, confession, and repentance can be challenging. However, this collect reminds us of what truly leads us to these practices: God's mercy. The Lord understands our frailty. He understands why we fall and when we fall into temptation and sin. With every fall, the Lord stands ready to catch us and to restore us. Paul wrote about this incredible mercy in his letter to the Romans: *"God's kindness is meant to lead you to repentance"* (Romans 2:4). God's law doesn't motivate us to do right; God's kindness, mercy, grace, and steadfast love are the inspirational encouragement for our devotion and good works.

Many of us have grown to believe that God is angry or disappointed with us. The cross speaks another message. God loves us and would do anything to save us from sin, death, and the work of the enemy. Through the cross of Christ, the love of God and the justice of God were perfectly demonstrated. God provided a perfect payment for sin through his beloved Son and God's justice was perfectly satisfied through the shed blood of Jesus.

God longs to embrace you in your place of fallenness and sin. He longs to draw you near, to cover you in the righteousness of Jesus Christ, and to restore you to all the fullness of who he made you to be.

Hearts become soft and broken when they are secure in love. As we enter this second week of Lent, how would the Lord ask you to experience his grace? How could you let go of the need to perform, the guilt, and the condemnation to embrace the invitation of the cross?

The cross summons you to come to God just as you are. As you experience the steadfast love of God and the abundant grace made available through Jesus Christ, you will honestly see the sin that holds you and acknowledge the temptations that seem to linger. Invite the Lord into those places. Ask him to give you his perspective on that sin and those temptations then allow his grace to pour over you so that you can be made clean, righteous, and healed.

Penitence comes not through self-abasement but through the steadfast love of the Savior. Transformation then happens through the power of the Holy Spirit working in you and through you not as a result of your own hard work or discipline. Lent is the holy invitation to truly look at the love of God demonstrated on the cross of Jesus Christ then to look within yourself. Does he have more for you? Does he want to set you free from habits, ways of thinking, or behaviors? God loves you with a perfect and steadfast love. In that love, he wants to set you free from all that hinders you from fully living as his beloved child.

When you live as that beloved child, he is truly glorified!

Reflection:

How is the Lord calling you to experience his mercy today? Rest in that mercy, allow it to break your heart over sin, and then ask the Lord to cleanse, heal, and restore you. He is for you!

The Lord's Agenda
Monday

"And he began to teach them that the Son of Man must suffer many things and be rejected by the elders and the chief priests and the scribes and be killed, and after three days rise again. And he said this plainly. And Peter took him aside and began to rebuke him. But turning and seeing his disciples, he rebuked Peter and said, 'Get behind me, Satan! For you are not setting your mind on the things of God, but on the things of man.'" Mark 8:31-33

To truly appreciate these words of Jesus, we need to look back at the events recorded earlier in this narrative. Jesus and his disciples had been hard at work. Jesus had been teaching, healing, and then feeding the more than four thousand people who had gathered around him for ministry. Meanwhile, the disciples had been assisting Jesus, passing out food, and absorbing the teachings of Jesus. After the miraculous feeding, Jesus was questioned by the Pharisees, then he miraculously healed a blind man. As Jesus and the disciples walked towards Caesarea Philippi, Jesus then asked the disciples two questions: "Who do people say that I am?" and "Who do you say that I am?" Peter made his great profession, "You are the Christ" (Mark 8:27-30).

The disciples had experienced the power of Jesus, the brilliance of Jesus, and the assurance that Jesus was the promised Messiah. How amazing it must have been to see the kingdom of God revealed before their eyes. Unfortunately, everyone, including the disciples, had a plan for Jesus which did not align with the Lord's plan. Each of these agendas unraveled as Jesus told the disciples of his upcoming rejection, death, and resurrection.

Peter, feeling quite confident in himself after the great confession and Jesus' affirmation of him, challenged Jesus on this plan of suffering, death, and resurrection. That could never happen to Jesus! He was the Messiah; he was the true king of Israel; and he was to establish his earthly kingdom in which there would be peace for the nation of Israel as well as new power. In focusing on his own agenda, Peter did not see God's agenda for Jesus. Jesus' response surely jolted Peter. He went from being called the rock to being called Satan (See Matthew 16:13-23). Jesus called Peter to abandon his agenda and to embrace the Lord's agenda. To be a disciple of Jesus was to see as God sees and not as man sees.

Isn't that our challenge still today? We make plans for our lives, and we want the Lord to fully cooperate with our plans. When he directs us in a different way or deliberately closes doors, we fuss and whine. However, the Lord calls us to see with his eyes and to embrace his agenda which often means leaving our own plans behind us.

The season of Lent is an opportune time to lay our agendas before the Lord, to ask him if we are seeing what he wants us to see and pursuing what he wants us to pursue. When the Lord challenges and redirects us, it is always for a better plan. He longs to grow us into faithful kingdom builders.

Reflection:

Are you embracing God's agenda or holding onto your own? What would the Lord ask you to surrender to him today?

Take Up Your Cross and Follow Me
Tuesday

"And calling the crowd to him with his disciples, he said to them, 'If anyone would come after me, let him deny himself and take up his cross and follow me. For whoever would save his life will lose it, but whoever loses his life for my sake and the gospel's will save it. For what does it profit a man to gain the whole world and forfeit his soul? For what can a man give in return for his soul? For whoever is ashamed of me and of my words in this adulterous and sinful generation, of him will the Son of Man also be ashamed when he comes in the glory of his Father with the holy angels.'" Mark 8:34-38

The private conversation between Jesus and his disciples has gone public. Jesus went from telling the disciples about his upcoming rejection, death, and resurrection to teaching the crowds about what it meant to follow him. Until now, following Jesus meant free food, healings, and great teaching. However, there would be much more to becoming a disciple of Jesus Christ. Unbeknownst to them, the disciples were following Jesus to the cross.

This trek to the cross was not one of comfort or self-promotion. Instead, Jesus would demonstrate true humility. In the Garden of Gethsemane, Jesus would plead with the Father to take the cup from him. He knew the way ahead would be excruciating. Yet, Jesus continued to surrender to the will of the Father. Those who wanted to follow Jesus would have to learn the same humility, surrender, and obedience.

Jesus knew that these disciples would face great persecution and even martyrdom after his ascension to the Father. The irony was that in dying on behalf of sin, Jesus made the way for all who would believe in him to have eternal life. Death led to life and not just one life but many lives.

The disciples and all the followers of Jesus would be called to also take up their cross and to follow Jesus on the path of death to self and life to the Lord. To refuse this invitation was to refuse a relationship with the triune God. Jesus was telling his followers that they could love their lives in this world and cling to the fleeting security found in the world or they could surrender their earthly comforts to pursue an eternal security found in Jesus Christ alone.

To proclaim the name of Jesus Christ as the Lord and Savior of the world may result in persecution and even death in this world. This proclamation would also guarantee eternal life with the Lord. To deny Jesus Christ as the Messiah may lead to earthly peace but will result in eternal separation from the Father. Comfort either in this world or in the world to come – Jesus said that every person must choose.

The season of Lent is that invitation to pick up your cross and to follow Jesus. It is also the time to examine whether you are dying daily to yourself to build the kingdom of God. The costs may be high in this world, but the payment will be much greater in eternity!

Reflection:

How is Jesus calling you to pick up your cross today?

The Lord Hears the Cries of His People
Wednesday

"I will tell of your name to my brothers; in the midst of the congregation I will praise you: You who fear the Lord, praise him! All you offspring of Jacob, glorify him, and stand in awe of him, all you offspring of Israel! For he has not despised or abhorred the affliction of the afflicted, and he has not hidden his face from him, but has heard, when he cried to him. From you comes my praise in the great congregation; my vows I will perform before those who fear him. The afflicted shall eat and be satisfied; those who seek him shall praise the Lord! May your hearts live forever!" Psalm 22:22-26

In this psalm, King David called himself and his readers to put their full confidence in God. If you read through the entirety of the psalm, it is not all praise and adoration. Instead, the psalm begins with David questioning God: *"My God, my God, why have you forsaken me?"* (Psalm 22:1). David felt abandoned and attacked. He desperately needed the presence, power, and vindication of the Lord. In his weakness, David cried out to the one who was strong. He put his trust in God even when circumstances were challenging and out of his control.

That trust led to praise. Circumstances had not yet changed, but David knew the character and faithfulness of God. David remembered the many ways in which the Lord had worked on his behalf in the past. David remembered God's faithfulness and chose to put his trust in the Lord once again. Trusting God led David to praise him. In praising the Lord, David found strength and hope. He would tell the nation of Israel of God's deliverance. David had confidence that he would gather again in corporate worship of the Lord with his people.

What enabled David to express such confidence in the Lord? He knew that God listened to the cries of his people. The Lord did not despise the weakness of David but answered these desperate prayers. The Lord was not one to hide but was ever present and active in the lives of his children. This all powerful and all-knowing God loved to care for his children; he delighted in rescuing them and providing for them: *"The afflicted shall eat and be satisfied"* (v. 26). David trusted that the Lord saw him, heard him, and would vindicate him.

David's confidence in the Lord inspired his followers to also place their confidence in the Lord. Though king of Israel, David had no pretenses before the Lord. He lamented his condition and cried to the Lord for help. David allowed himself to be broken so that in the strength of the Lord he could be restored.

Isn't that the invitation of Lent? To come authentically before the Lord without any pretenses, coverings, or excuses and to declare your need for the Lord. In your flesh, you are weak but in God's Spirit, you can be made strong. You are called to honestly lament so that you can honestly praise and worship. That praise and worship of the Lord, remembering who he is and what he has done, allows you to come into alignment with his love, grace, and power.

The Lord still loves to answer the cries of his children!

Reflection:

Will you follow David's example in the practice of lamenting, crying out, and worshipping?

God's Call
Thursday

"When Abram was ninety-nine years old the Lord appeared to Abram and said to him, 'I am God Almighty; walk before me, and be blameless, that I may make my covenant between me and you, and may multiply you greatly.' Then Abram fell on his face. And God said to him, 'Behold, my covenant is with you, and you shall be the father of a multitude of nations. No longer shall your name be called Abram, but your name shall be Abraham, for I have made you the father of a multitude of nations. I will make you exceedingly fruitful, and I will make you into nations, and kings shall come from you. And I will establish my covenant between me and you and your offspring after you throughout their generations for an everlasting covenant, to be God to you and to your offspring after you.'" Genesis 17:1-7

This was not God's first encounter with Abram. In chapter 12, the Lord called Abram to leave his land and to follow the Lord to a new land. There, the Lord would make a great nation from Abram. With radical faith, Abram obeyed the Lord and followed him to this new land and new opportunity. Despite Abram's obedience, the way ahead wasn't always clear or easy. Abram made a few concessions to save his skin as he told the Egyptians that Sarai was his sister and not his wife (Genesis 12:10-20). When God did not fulfill his promise for a son in Abram's timing (or Sarai's timing), Abram and Sarai took matters into their own hands. Abram slept with Sarai's maid Hagar, and Ishmael was conceived. As we get to chapter 17, God reaffirms his call to Abram and then changes Abram's name to Abraham. Again, God promises that Abraham and Sarah (Sarai's name changed, too) would conceive and bear a son. From this son, God would build the nations.

What did Abram do to deserve this calling of the Lord and these glorious promises? He was just a man, a man who didn't always make the best choices. He was married but had no children. His future wasn't looking all that bright. Abram did nothing to deserve this favor and kindness of the Lord. He was chosen to be the father of many nations. He was chosen to follow the Lord then equipped to obey. Abram was a fallen man who received the grace of God and the call of God. There was nothing remarkable about Abram except that he responded in faith.

True to his word, God fulfilled his promises to Abraham through the miraculous conception and birth of Isaac. What was thought to be dead became a great source of life as the nation of Israel was also born.

Like Abram, we are chosen by the Lord and called to follow him in faith. We become the recipients of God's covenantal promises. We aren't given these promises because of what we have done or will do. We are given these promises through God's call on our lives. Not only does God call us, but he equips us to follow him in faith and obedience through the gift of the Holy Spirit. Through us, God wants to create something glorious. He has people for us to evangelize and disciple, ministries for us to build, kingdom work that is uniquely designed for us.

Do we respond as Abram did, or do we allow our mistakes and failures to hinder us and hold us back from this great calling? Just as God changed Abram's name to Abraham, so he wants to change our names – from fearful to trusting, from shame to righteousness, from timid to bold, from dead to alive in Christ.

Reflection:

Are you embracing God's call on your life? What would the Lord have you learn from Abraham?

God's Faithfulness
Friday

"He did not weaken in faith when he considered his own body, which was as good as dead (since he was about a hundred years old), or when he considered the barrenness of Sarah's womb. No unbelief made him waver concerning the promise of God, but he grew strong in his faith as he gave glory to God, fully convinced that God was able to do what he had promised." Romans 4:19-21

How did Abraham develop such strong faith? Paul says that he did not weaken in his faith, nor did he doubt in God's ability to carry out what he had promised. How did Abraham believe in full confidence that God would do what he said?

It could be said that belief was easier for Abraham, simply because God had spoken directly to him. This is true, yet Abraham still had no reason to trust God. Don't we doubt the voices of those who make promises to us? God's Word cannot be compared to human promises, but our sinful nature has the tendency of equating the two, leading us to doubt God. Paul also points out that Abraham's faith was not due to his circumstances, because God's promises were impossible considering Abraham and Sarah's physical conditions. For how could a barren woman give birth to an entire nation?

Perhaps Abraham's faith stemmed from his response to God. When God called him, Abraham immediately acted and obeyed the command. He never hesitated, but fully gave himself over to the will and purposes of the One who called him. The writer of Hebrews denotes Abraham as being a member of the hall of faith; defining faith as *"the assurance of things hoped for, the conviction of things not seen"* (Heb. 11:1). Thus, Abraham chose belief in response to the conviction of the Holy Spirit.

There can be many takeaways from the story of Abraham, one of them being the importance of identifying and responding to conviction. This is a righteous prompting from the Holy Spirit to align with the will of God; however, conviction from the devil can be shameful manipulation disguised as discipline.

Like Abraham, we must be able to determine the direction of God in our lives through conviction, as well as trust that God is exactly who he says that he is. The Bible, history, and our lives serve as a testament that God's faithfulness will never cease. All that we can offer God is our heart and our belief, just like Abraham. Through the blood of Jesus, our faith will be counted to us as righteousness too.

Reflection:

What is your response to this? Where can you see God's faithfulness in your life? What convictions have you felt from the Holy Spirit recently? I encourage you to test your conviction with scripture and see if it aligns with the character of God. If you are certain of the direction of God, then respond in faith like Abraham by choosing obedience.

The Gift of Imperfection
Saturday

"That is why [Abraham's] faith was 'counted to him as righteousness.' But the words 'it was counted to him' were not written for his sake alone, but for ours also. It will be counted to us who believe in him who raised from the dead Jesus our Lord, who was delivered up for our trespasses and raised for our justification." Romans 4:22-25

Brené Brown wrote an enlightening book entitled *The Gifts of Imperfection: Let Go of Who You Think You're Supposed to Be and Embrace Who You Are.* Just the title of this book is challenging and yet inspiring. Are there really gifts to our imperfections? Those things which we hold up as our great failures, are there redeeming characteristics or things that God will do through our perceived failures?

Abraham was chosen and called to be the father of many nations. He obeyed but not perfectly. He lied. He laughed at the promises of God. He doubted at times. He committed adultery to try and produce the promised heir. Abraham was not righteous on his own; Abraham was declared righteous through his faith in God. This righteousness was a gift from God; it was not something that Abraham earned through his own merits and work.

Abraham is remembered not for all these imperfections but for his faith and the righteousness credited to him through that faith. God used Abraham despite his imperfections. Abraham did not consistently look back to all that he had done wrong, but he continued to walk with the Lord and to choose faith. His imperfections were a gift because they pointed beyond himself. Abraham alone was not the father of many nations. Instead, Abraham, through the call and work of God, was the father of many nations. Abraham was not perfect, but the one who called him was perfect.

Paul referred to Abraham as an example of imputed righteousness. Like Abraham, we all struggle with imperfections; we all fall short of the glory of God. However, through faith in the salvific work of Jesus Christ on the cross, we become the righteousness of Christ. Through the waters of baptism, we die to our sin nature, and we are resurrected to our new nature in Christ--the nature that is holy, new, and fully righteous. We are justified through Christ, meaning that we are made perfectly clean, whole, and holy. When the Lord looks at us, he does not see our sin; he sees the righteousness of his Son. What an amazing gift!

The gift of our imperfection is that it reveals our need for a Savior. We cannot cleanse ourselves, fix ourselves, or heal ourselves. Thankfully, God can and will do all those things. Our imperfections are our invitations to come humbly before him, to confess the ways in which we have gone astray, to ask for forgiveness for those sins, then to experience power through the Holy Spirit to turn from sin.

Reflection:

How do you view your sin and imperfections? How would the Lord have you view them?

Week of the Third Sunday in Lent

True Power Comes from the Lord
Sunday

"Almighty God, you know that we have no power in ourselves to help ourselves: Keep us both outwardly in our bodies and inwardly in our souls, that we may be defended from all adversities which may happen to the body, and from all evil thoughts which may assault and hurt the soul; through Jesus Christ our Lord, who lives and reigns with you and the Holy Spirit, one God, for ever and ever. Amen." Collect for the Third Sunday in Lent, BCP

We are dependent people! While the world will tell us over and over again how powerful we are, how wise we are, and how independent we can be, the Lord will tell us a different story. In fact, every gift of wisdom, strength, and ability we have comes from the Creator God. We are designed to live in relationship to him. We are designed to surrender these gifts to him and to allow him to guide us in his ways and plans. Our gifts are not for our glory but for his glory.

We have no power in ourselves except that which has been given to us by the Lord. We certainly have no power in ourselves to save ourselves. While we are people made in the image of God, our sin has marred that image, and we fall short of the glory of God. The Lord would have us look whole-heartedly to him for the gift of salvation as well as for guidance and empowerment to lead lives of holiness.

Do we daily pray for guidance and empowerment, or do we seek to live in our own power? The prayer of our Collect today is that we would recognize our need for the Lord and that we would turn to him not just for salvation but for guidance, protection, and divine wisdom.

May we surrender our hearts and our minds to him today. May we know his hand of protection over our lives as well as his transformative work in our minds. When we recognize our weakness, God can become strong in us and through us.

Reflection:

How would the Lord have you look to him today for strength, direction, and transformation?

Holy and Right Worship of the Lord
Monday

"The Passover of the Jews was at hand, and Jesus went up to Jerusalem. In the temple he found those who were selling oxen and sheep and pigeons, and the money-changers sitting there. And making a whip of cords, he drove them all out of the temple, with the sheep and oxen. And he poured out the coins of the money-changers and overturned their tables. And he told those who sold the pigeons, 'Take these things away; do not make my Father's house a house of trade.' His disciples remembered that it was written, 'Zeal for your house will consume me.'"
John 2:13-17

The Jewish people were in full preparation for the celebration of the Passover. People from all over would travel to Jerusalem for this holy day. For those who traveled great distances, it was much more difficult to bring their offerings along with them; therefore, merchants would set up shops in the outer courts of the temple. Unfortunately, this market was not always done with purity of heart. Merchants would overcharge for these animals, and many of the animals would have defects that were not allowed in the sacrificial offerings. In other words, they took advantage of the people's need and used it as an opportunity to make a nice profit. Even places of worship can become places of commerce.

A new side of Jesus emerges in this narrative. Instead of the meek, compassionate Jesus, we encounter his holy anger. For the nation of Israel, the temple was the dwelling place of God. It was a place to offer sacrifices on behalf of the sins of the people and to worship God. As Jesus walked into the outer courts, he saw a holy place defiled by the greed of man. Righteous anger consumed Jesus as he drove out the money-changers and all their animals.

While Jesus was patient and kind, Jesus was also passionate for the Lord. He modelled what it meant to love the Lord with all his heart, soul, and mind. Jesus was fully devoted to his Father, and he perfectly demonstrated his devotion. Where this anger of Jesus may shock us as it surely shocked the people of his day, we are called to examine our approach to worship. Do we waltz into church on Sundays with an agenda to impress our brothers and sisters, to make business connections, or to simply be taught and engaged?

Worship is not about what we receive; worship is about offering our hearts, minds, and spirits to the Lord. It is a time to forget about ourselves and to seek the Lord, to listen to his words spoken through the reading of Scripture, to receive his teaching through the sermon, to make our offering through the tithe, and to receive the fullness of his grace through communion. Worship is not about us; worship is all about the Lord.

Imagine Jesus walking into your church on Sunday. What would he say to you personally about your heart towards worship? This season of Lent is a time to move out of our normal practices of faith to see if God has something more, something greater in mind for us. Worship is about meeting with a holy God, allowing him to search us and know us, then to lead us into self-examination through grace.

May we turn from any unholy practices in our places of worship or in our posture of worship so that we can surrender ourselves to the Lord.

Reflection:

How would the Lord like to challenge you in the way you worship?

Recognizing the Messiah
Tuesday

"So the Jews said to him, 'What sign do you show us for doing these things?' Jesus answered them, 'Destroy this temple, and in three days I will raise it up.' The Jews then said, 'It has taken forty-six years to build this temple, and will you raise it up in three days?' But he was speaking about the temple of his body. When therefore he was raised from the dead, his disciples remembered that he had said this, and they believed the Scripture and the word that Jesus had spoken." John 2:18-22

Since the fall of Adam and Eve in the garden, the people of God had been awaiting the Messiah. The nation of Israel looked to that day when the Lord would come and live among his people, a day when his kingdom would be established in this world. Ironically, though they had looked forward to that day and prayed fervently for the Messiah's coming, they did not recognize the Son of God when he finally came.

In our reading for today, Jesus had just cleared the temple of the money-changers and all their animals for sale. There was certainly great confusion and chaos as these people and animals ran from the temple. The leaders were dumbfounded as their preparations for the Passover were being thwarted. Why would Jesus disrupt all that they had done and practiced through the years?

With the coming of the Messiah to dwell among his people as a man, everything had to change! For years, the temple was the place to meet with the Lord, to worship, and to make offerings unto him. Now, the temple was not the dwelling place of God; Jesus was the dwelling place of God. Sadly, the people were so consumed with how things had been that they missed the presence of God standing right before them. God was made manifest through the person of Jesus. Jesus revealed the Father in everything that he did: preaching, teaching, healing, feeding the multitudes, and living among his people.

In revealing the Father, Jesus also revealed the hearts of mankind. Were they truly seeking God in his temple, or were they going through the motions? Jesus' actions and words that day were intended to shake them from their slumber and help them to look beyond what had been to what was right before their eyes. He challenged them to destroy the temple and he would rebuild it in three days. Their response revealed that they believed he was speaking of the temple building, when Jesus was actually speaking of his body, the true dwelling place of God.

How do we miss the person and work of Jesus today? How do we get consumed with the way things are or the way we think things should be and completely miss the invitation to experience the Lord? Are we missing the work of the Lord as it happens before our very eyes? The season of Lent is designed to shake us from our slumber, from all the ways that we start gliding through life and the practice of our Christian faith. May we turn from what was or how we think things should be and embrace the person of Jesus Christ as he is. He won't always work according to our plans, but his plans will always be very good.

Reflection:

How are your Lenten disciplines awakening you to the presence of the Lord, the work of the Lord, and the invitation of the Lord to come deeper into the knowledge, love, and worship of him?

The Foolishness of God
Wednesday

"For the word of the cross is folly to those who are perishing, but to us who are being saved it is the power of God. For it is written, 'I will destroy the wisdom of the wise, and the discernment of the discerning I will thwart.' Where is the one who is wise? Where is the scribe? Where is the debater of this age? Has not God made foolish the wisdom of the world? For since, in the wisdom of God, the world did not know God through wisdom, it pleased God through the folly of what we preach to save those who believe. For Jews demand signs and Greeks seek wisdom, but we preach Christ crucified, a stumbling block to Jews and folly to Gentiles, but to those who are called, both Jews and Greeks, Christ the power of God and the wisdom of God. For the foolishness of God is wiser than men, and the weakness of God is stronger than men."
1 Corinthians 1:18-25

In the ancient world, the cross was a symbol of death, humiliation, and excruciating pain. It was the cruelest form of death imaginable to people at that time. To think that the salvation of mankind could be accomplished through death on a cross was absurdity. Why would a sinless man die a sinner's death on a cross?

Paul speaks with his typical clarity. The ways of God are not the ways of man! God's ways will challenge those who think themselves to be wise as he will call them to full humility. To receive the gifts of God, one must die to the wisdom of the world and embrace the wisdom of God. That means that to the world, they may appear quite foolish. Jesus taught that to be his disciple, one had to pick up his or her cross and follow him (Matthew 16:24). Die to self in order to live to the Lord.

Isn't that the daily call of our Christian faith, especially in the season of Lent? We are called to move out of our comfortable ways of living and to embrace 40 days of self-denial and self-examination. While the rest of the world looks forward to the Easter Bunny's visit, the Christian looks to the pain and humiliation of Good Friday as the means to the greatest celebration on Easter morning.

How do you receive the call to humility, the call to pick up your cross, and the call to follow Jesus to Calvary? Have you surrendered your wisdom? What about your plans? Are you willing to truly embrace the foolishness of the cross with faith that resurrection power awaits you?

Paul, the Hebrew of Hebrews, the one who had studied under the greatest teachers of the Jewish faith, gave everything up to follow Jesus. He exemplified what it meant to surrender the wisdom of the world to embrace the foolishness of the cross. Paul would challenge you today to consider what God's call looks like for your life and whether you are truly surrendering to this call. Paul would also remind you that obedience to the Lord doesn't always look successful in the eyes of man but will lead to the greatest rewards imaginable: *"For the foolishness of God is wiser than men, and the weakness of God is stronger than men"* (v. 25).

Reflection:

Is there something of great worldly value that the Lord would have you to surrender unto him in order to fully embrace his call on your life?

The Glory of God Revealed for You
Thursday

"The heavens declare the glory of God, and the sky above proclaims his handiwork. Day to day pours out speech, and night to night reveals knowledge. There is no speech, nor are there words, whose voice is not heard. Their voice goes out through all the earth, and their words to the end of the world." Psalm 19:1-4

Does God truly reveal himself to his people? Since Adam and Eve, we read about God revealing himself. He walked in the garden with Adam and Eve; he gave them specific instructions as to how they were to live in the garden. He spoke to Abram of the plans he had for him, the plans to move him from his homeland to a new land in which he would build a great nation. God astounded Moses in the burning bush as he spoke to Moses of who he was, how he saw the oppression of his people, and then how he would use Moses to rescue his people. In the tabernacle, God dwelt among his people and showcased his glory, then there was the temple, and then there was the greatest display of glory in the person of Jesus Christ.

God loves to make himself known. That is why we have the pages of Scripture packed full of narratives that teach about God and about what it means to live as a child of God. Beyond Scripture, the Lord reveals himself through the glory of his creation. Paul would write that men are without excuse: *"For his invisible attributes, namely, his eternal power and divine nature, have been clearly perceived, ever since the creation of the world, in the things that have been made"* (Romans 1:20). Even without words, the glory of God is clearly evident in his creation. God blesses us each day with light then darkness. He provides water for the earth, glorious sunsets, mountain ridges, oceans filled with amazing creatures. God is abundantly creative and expresses himself through all that he has made.

We must ask ourselves if we have eyes to see and hearts to receive his revelation. Or are we too busy or self-consumed to notice the glory of God that surrounds us? Chris Tomlin sings about God's expression to us in creation: "…Morning, I see you in the sunrise every morning. It's like a picture that you've painted for me. A love letter in the sky" (Nobody Loves Me Like You). Chris goes on to say that this revelation of God creates awe and wonder within him that leads him to worship and marvel in God's love for him. Chris Tomlin delights in reading God's love letter and invites us to do the same.

"The heavens declare the glory of God, and the sky above proclaims his handiwork" (v. 1). How is God calling you to slow down and to take notice of his glory and handiwork? What is your holy invitation through this Lenten season to receive his love for you displayed? When we have eyes to see and a heart to receive, all of creation tells us the glory of God, the goodness of God, the provision of God, and the love of God. May we stop, may we see, and may we receive the fullness of his revelation!

Reflection:

Do you see nature as a reflection of God's glory and a love letter that God writes to you each morning?

The Way of the Lord
Friday

"The law of the Lord is perfect, reviving the soul; the testimony of the Lord is sure, making wise the simple; the precepts of the Lord are right, rejoicing the heart; the commandment of the Lord is pure, enlightening the eyes; the fear of the Lord is clean, enduring forever; the rules of the Lord are true, and righteous altogether." **Psalm 19:7-9**

In the six preceding verses of Psalm 19, David wrote of how God reveals himself through his creation and how that creation displays his glory throughout the world. As we move into these next few verses, David wrote of how God reveals himself through his law, testimony, precepts, and commandments. The glory of the Lord was also revealed through each of these as was his moral perfection and purity. We are called to marvel at God through his creation then to worship and adore him. That worship and adoration would naturally lead one to want to know God better, to enjoy relationship with him, and to seek to live in alignment with his will.

David declared that the law of the Lord is perfect and revives the soul. When we live our lives according to God's perfect law, we love the things that God loves, and we enjoy the benefits of obedience. Our souls are revived as they are not weighed down by the weight of sin and the consequences of that sin.

The testimony of the Lord is sure and makes the simple person wise. Trusting in God's words allows understanding of the divine, of things that far surpass our human understanding. God's truth enlightens us to know him, to understand him, and to articulate his will and ways.

The precepts of the Lord are right and cause our hearts to rejoice. When we allow God to guide us according to his plans and purposes, we find joy. David understood that when he allowed God to guide his decisions and actions, he was able to remain close to the Lord. There was safety and comfort in his obedience as well as great joy.

Lastly, the commandment of the Lord is pure and enlightens the eyes. Obeying the commandment of the Lord kept one from sinning and allowed him to walk faithfully in the light of the Lord. Thus, there was clarity and awareness.

All these – the law, testimony, precept, and commandment – they look back to the Mosaic covenant and to God's plan for how his people were to live. God has such good plans for his people. When we choose obedience to his will and ways, we can enjoy those plans – our souls are revived; we are made wise; our hearts rejoice; and our eyes are enlightened. Are you experiencing these things in your life and in your relationship with the Lord?

Often, we doubt the Lord. We doubt his goodness, and we think that his rules are there to restrict us or to hinder our joy. The Lord would have us understand that the opposite is true. All his commandments are there to lead us into life, into the fullness of life that God has for us.

Reflection:

How do you view the laws and teachings of the Lord? Is there anything he may be calling you to surrender today so that you can live faithfully before him and so that he can lead you into the fullness of joy and life?

The Sweet Rewards of Obedience
Saturday

"The law of the Lord is perfect, reviving the soul; the testimony of the Lord is sure, making wise the simple; the precepts of the Lord are right, rejoicing the heart; the commandment of the Lord is pure, enlightening the eyes; the fear of the Lord is clean, enduring forever; the rules of the Lord are true, and righteous altogether. More to be desired are they than gold, even much fine gold; sweeter also than honey and drippings of the honeycomb. Moreover, by them is your servant warned; in keeping them is great reward." **Psalm 19:7-11**

David wrote that God's law was to be desired even more than gold, even the finest of gold. To live in obedience to the Lord meant much more to David than even the greatest wealth in this world. David had an understanding that nothing in this world could compare to the love of the Lord and the joy of living in relationship with him. David also must have grasped how the things of this world are temporary while the things of God are eternal.

Is that how we view our wealth? Is that how we view our lives? Do we lay aside our temporary delights to seek eternal delights? Maybe that looks like turning from a pattern of sin to pursue a pattern of holiness. Maybe that means faithfully setting aside every Sunday to worship the Lord instead of heading to the golf course or staying in pajamas. Maybe that means surrendering your grip on finances and truly tithing from what God has entrusted to you.

Whatever God has called you to do, David will remind you that his ways are sweeter than anything you can enjoy on this earth. There are great experiences here, and the Lord would have you enjoy them; however, your enjoyment is so greatly enhanced when it is from a place of obedience. To enjoy one's spouse as opposed to another is so much greater; the Lord loves to bless the covenant of marriage. To enjoy one serving of ice cream is so much greater than finishing the carton, and the scale won't reflect your misdeeds the following day.

Life is much more enjoyable when you are not consumed with guilt and shame. God's ways are always sweeter than the ways of this world!

David concludes this section of his psalm with the reminder that fearing the Lord is healthy. David personally knew the pain of disobedience to the Lord. He experienced incredible heartache as a result of his disobedience, heartache that continued all throughout a very successful reign as King of Israel. David would call you to choose faithfulness so that you can be spared the consequences of sin and enjoy the blessings of obedience. The blessings of obedience are for eternity as well as for today.

Reflection:

How is the Lord challenging you today from David's psalm? How would he like to change your mindset concerning his laws and commandments? How would he have you change your thinking and your behavior?

Week of the Fourth Sunday in Lent

The Impatience of God's People
Sunday

"From Mount Hor they set out by the way to the Red Sea, to go around the land of Edom. And the people became impatient on the way. And the people spoke against God and against Moses, 'Why have you brought us up out of Egypt to die in the wilderness? For there is no food and no water, and we loathe this worthless food.'" Numbers 21:4-5

At this point in Israel's history, they have been traveling with God and Moses for many years. The nation of Israel has just miraculously defeated the Canaanites in battle. Though they have seen the hand of God rescue them from the land of Egypt, provide water and food, and overcome their enemies, yet the nation of Israel is still hard-hearted, lacking in faith, and set on their selfish desires.

God has provided everything they have needed – maybe not everything they have wanted but everything they have needed. Instead of living in worship and gratitude, the people make demands – for food, for water, for God and Moses to provide as they want them to. The text tells us that they became impatient. Surely, they were ready to settle in the promised land and to feel a sense of security and rest.

Once again, it is important to remember that it is their lack of obedience that has them *still* on the move. As a nation, Israel has not learned how to trust in the Lord and to obey him.

I wonder how we get impatient with the Lord today. Though we have seen his goodness over and over again in our lives, though we have experienced his provision for our every need (not every want), we continue to grumble against his plans, his ways, and… his timing.

We doubt God instead of trusting God; we rebel against him instead of surrendering to him and obeying him. Instead of enjoying an intimate relationship with the Lord and then enjoying his many gifts in our lives, we doubt him and try to do things in our own power, our own way, and in our own timing.

God's ways are not our ways; God's ways are always much greater than our ways! The Lord is worthy of our trust and our obedience. Like the nation of Israel in the wilderness, we can make the choice of whether to grumble and complain about what is lacking or to embrace what God is doing today.

May we choose the latter. This season of Lent, may we discipline ourselves to surrender, to wait, and to give thanks in all things. God has given us all things, including his one and only Son that we may have life through him. Let's embrace that life, trusting and obeying him through all of it.

Reflection:

Are there ways in which you are impatient with the Lord's work in your life or in the world today? What would the Lord want you to know? What does it look like for you to surrender, trust, and obey?

Obedience Leads to Life and Healing
Monday

"Then the Lord sent fiery serpents among the people, and they bit the people, so that many people of Israel died. And the people came to Moses and said, 'We have sinned, for we have spoken against the Lord and against you. Pray to the Lord, that he take away the serpents from us.' So Moses prayed for the people. And the Lord said to Moses, 'Make a fiery serpent and set it on a pole, and everyone who is bitten, when he sees it, shall live.' So Moses made a bronze serpent and set it on a pole. And if a serpent bit anyone, he would look at the bronze serpent and live."
Numbers 21:6-9

Last week in the Gospel reading, we saw Jesus clear the temple of the moneychangers and those who were selling animals to be sacrificed to God. Jesus demonstrated holy anger against the sin and greed of those who were taking advantage of God's people and using a place of worship as a place of commerce. Today, we read again of righteous anger towards sin and how that is demonstrated.

The nation of Israel was once again complaining against God and Moses. In times of impatience or frustration, the people asked why God had led them out of their bondage in Egypt to die in the wilderness. The first time they posed that question it was understandable. The Egyptian army was pursuing them with vigor and force, and the Israelites were trapped by the Red Sea behind them and the Egyptian army in front of them.

Who could have imagined that God would open the waters of the Red Sea for them to pass through it? Now however, after all these years of seeing God's miraculous work on their behalf, their question was ridiculous. They hadn't died; they were still alive. The problem was not with God or with Moses; the problem was the people. Instead of being grateful for all that they had received, they constantly demanded more and were never satisfied.

Clearly, God was angry at their self-centered whininess, and he sent fiery serpents to come among them. That would have surely gotten their attention. Not only were these serpents within their camp, but they would bite the people and even kill the people. After some time with the fiery snakes, the Israelites came to their senses. They realized they had sinned against God and against Moses. Once again, they realized that they could not save themselves, so they asked Moses to pray to the Lord to take away the serpents.

The Lord heard the prayer of Moses. We do not read that he took away the serpents but that the Lord provided healing for those who had been bitten. God instructed Moses to make a fiery serpent and to set it on a pole. Moses obeyed God; he crafted a serpent out of bronze, put in on a pole, and provided it for the people to see in their time of need. Notice how Moses obeys. He doesn't question the Lord about why another serpent or how a bronze serpent on a pole will heal people. Moses does what the Lord tells him to do. Because of his obedience, the Israelites find healing.

Obedience leads to life, to healing. While he was not perfect in obeying God, Moses does model what it means to hear from the Lord and to then obey the Lord. What are you to learn from his example? How is the Lord leading you to move out of your own selfish desires and demands to listen to him, to surrender to him, and to obey him?

Reflection:

Do you believe that obedience to God brings life and healing? How would the Lord like to minister to you today?

The Call to Look Up
Tuesday

"And as Moses lifted up the serpent in the wilderness, so must the Son of Man be lifted up, that whoever believes in him may have eternal life." John 3:14-15

In Numbers 21, we read of the Israelites grumbling against God's provision for them in the wilderness followed by God's judgement of them through fiery serpents within the camp. When they recognized their sin, the Israelites asked Moses to cry out to the Lord on their behalf. God's mercy was demonstrated through the serpent on the pole. When the people looked at the serpent lifted up on the pole, they found healing from the poisonous and life-threatening bites of the serpents. Salvation was found only by looking from themselves to the provision of God for them.

In our reading from the Gospel of John, John alludes to this serpent that was lifted up in the wilderness for the healing of God's people. Once again, to find healing the people must look away from themselves and up to the provision of God. To have eternal life, one must see and believe in the Son of Man who was lifted up on the cross. There the sin of mankind met with the justice of a holy God. In offering himself as the perfect sacrifice for sin, Jesus made the way for those who would believe in him to have eternal life.

God provided the serpent for the nation of Israel after they recognized their sin against him and against Moses. The Lord provided healing from his judgement and death from the serpents. Once again, God has provided healing; however, in order to receive the healing and the gift of eternal life, one must first recognize his or her need for salvation and the fact that there is no way to save oneself.

You need a Savior; I need a Savior. God has provided that Savior by sending his Son. The question becomes whether we will look to him. We are very good at surrounding ourselves with the comforts of this world and with many assurances that we are good people doing good things. The ongoing temptation of our comfortable lives is that we can do it on our own.

The invitation of Lent is to see that we are but dust, that we are mortal beings with limitations. If we could save ourselves, the Lord would not have sent his Son. Are you living in this holy invitation to see yourself, to see your sins and shortcomings, and to see your desperate need for a Savior? The gift of Easter is a glorious one when you have seen your need and God's great provision for your need.

May we lift our eyes to see the love of the Lord demonstrated on the cross for us and may we put our trust in his salvific work. When we believe in him, we too receive this gift of eternal life.

Reflection:

What does it mean for you to lift your eyes to see Jesus on the cross? How are you changed by what you see there?

God's Holy Invitation to You
Wednesday

"For God so loved the world, that he gave his only Son, that whoever believes in him should not perish but have eternal life. For God did not send his Son into the world to condemn the world, but in order that the world might be saved through him." John 3:16-17

John begins his Gospel much differently than Matthew, Mark, and Luke. As opposed to providing historical information about the genealogy of Jesus, the prophecy of Jesus, or the political background into which he was born, the apostle John looks back to the very beginning – to the Word that was God and was with God. This Word was made manifest in the person of Jesus Christ: *"In him was life, and the life was the light of men. The light shines in the darkness, and the darkness has not overcome it"* (John 1:4-5). John makes it very clear that Jesus is the eternal God who came to dwell among his people. The light of his divinity shown into the darkness revealing the glory of God and the sin of humanity.

In revealing the darkness of human sin, Jesus provided forgiveness and healing for that sin. Revelation of sin was intended to lead to redemption. How can one be redeemed from something of which he is completely unaware? Since the fall of Adam and Eve in the garden, humanity has had a sin problem. We know the right thing to do, but we often find ourselves unwilling or unable to do that right thing. Sin has a hold on us.

Jesus came to save us from that sin. Through him, we see sin but through him we also see the perfect payment for sin. Jesus came to show the love of his Father. God saw that mankind could not keep the law; he knew their desperate plight; and he had a perfect payment for sin provided through the death of his Son. Perfect love and perfect holiness demand justice. Justice was served as the perfect Son of God took the sin of the world upon his wounded body. His offering satisfied the wrath of a holy God.

When the Lord calls us to acknowledge our sin, it is not for the purpose of making us feel guilty or ashamed. Instead, it is a holy invitation to move from acknowledgement to confession, from confession to repentance, and from repentance into holy living. Jesus came that we could see our sin but not remain dead in our sin. Jesus came that we may have life, abundant life in this world and eternal life with the Father.

How do you receive this holy invitation to see your sin? Do you resist and retreat to a place of hiding or do you open yourself to see and to be seen? To see your sin is to see your need for salvation. Jesus wants to be your salvation, and he wants you to enjoy all the blessings and gifts of that salvation. Jesus came to save you – to save you from sin, from guilt, from condemnation, from death, and from all the forces of evil. Will you receive his gift for you and live free from the grip of sin?

Reflection:

When you think of conviction, do you think of salvation or condemnation? What is God's holy invitation to you today?

The Inclusion, Acceptance, and Tolerance of the Cross of Christ
Thursday

"Whoever believes in him is not condemned, but whoever does not believe is condemned already, because he has not believed in the name of the only Son of God. And this is the judgement: the light has come into the world, and people loved the darkness rather than the light because their works were evil. For everyone who does wicked things hates the light and does not come to the light, lest his works should be exposed. But whoever does what is true comes to the light, so that it may be clearly seen that his works have been carried out in God." John 3:18-21

There is eternal life and freedom from condemnation through trust in the Son of God; there is also condemnation for those who do not put their trust in his Son. This is not a popular message in our world today! The world longs for inclusion, acceptance, and tolerance of all things. Jesus came to include all people into his kingdom; salvation moved from the Jews to all the nations and all the peoples of this world. Anyone who would call upon the name of Jesus would be saved. All people were included in the invitation to live as children of God.

Jesus came to accept those who had been rejected. He welcomed the tax collectors and notorious sinners. He was known for even having dinner parties with such people. Contrary to the practices of his time, Jesus not only ministered to women, but he included them in his work of ministry. Mary and Martha were among his closest friends. Jesus welcomed the outcast of society; he touched and healed the lepers who were considered unclean. Jesus accepted all people who came to him.

Jesus tolerated sin, ignorance, and even the constant objections and accusations of his enemies. Jesus tolerated the onslaught of needs that were brought before him, the doubt of even his closest friends, and the humiliation of the cross.

The life of Jesus modelled inclusion, acceptance, and tolerance. However, Jesus was very clear that there was only one way to the Father and that was through him. Without faith in Jesus Christ, no one will be included in the kingdom of God; there will be no acceptance by the Father, as a holy God cannot tolerate sin. Jesus came to shine light into the darkness. The children of God will come to the light, walk in the light, and live in that light. Those who reject the Son of God choose to remain in darkness. They are the ones who are unwilling to acknowledge their sin and to receive the salvation offered through the cross of Jesus Christ.

The cross is the perfect invitation to be included, accepted, and even tolerated. However, the apostle John makes it very clear that to get to the Father, one must embrace the cross of Christ. That cross frees one from the condemnation of sin. That cross is the means to forgiveness and restoration. To reject the cross of Christ is to welcome condemnation for sin.

Light or darkness, forgiveness or condemnation, eternal life with the Father or eternal life with the devil – which will you choose to live into today?

Reflection:

Are you living in the light of the cross?

But God
Friday

"And you were dead in the trespasses and sins in which you once walked, following the course of this world, following the prince of the power of the air, the spirit that is now at work in the sons of disobedience – among whom we all once lived in the passions of our flesh, carrying out the desires of the body and the mind, and were by nature children of wrath, like the rest of mankind. But God, being rich in mercy, because of the great love with which he loved us, even when we were dead in our trespasses, made us alive together with Christ – by grace you have been saved – and raised us up with him and seated us with him in the heavenly place in Christ Jesus, so that in the coming ages he might show the immeasurable riches of his grace in kindness toward us in Christ Jesus." Ephesians 2:1-7

Paul writes to the church in Ephesus and to us today with some dire news – we were dead in our trespasses and sins. Our citizenship was not in heaven but with the prince of this earth. There really was no hope for any of us.

But God.

These are two of the most important words in the Bible. There is what we were in our own flesh and strength, but then there is what God made us to be through the gift of his Son. We were trapped in our pattern of sin, but now we have been rescued through the mercy and grace of God. Not only are we rescued from the pattern of sin and the destruction of sin, but God has now raised us up so that we can take our place in the heavenly realms with Jesus.

Notice the importance of those words – "But God." Not "But Brooke" or "Charlie", or "Allyson," or "William"... But God. On our own we could not achieve such an amazing gift. We will never be worthy of this mercy and grace of God. That is why it is called mercy; that is why it is called grace. It is undeserved and freely given from the Lord. Why did the Lord give us such an amazing gift? Paul says it is because of his great love for us.

Even in our trespasses and sins, the Lord loved us and had a rescue plan for us. What could be better than love that truly knows us, has seen all our failings and shortcomings, and yet makes the way clear for us to receive his mercy and grace? That is a steadfast and unconditional love that we humans have a hard time comprehending.

Whether we understand it or not, this steadfast love of the Lord is there beckoning us to come, to receive, and to live in the fullness of that love. Sadly, we sometimes resist the "But God" and insert the "But I" – But I am too broken, too sinful, too beyond redemption. Then there is the other extreme of "But I" – But I am a good person; I do my best and achieve great things; I am righteous or more righteous than others. Either way you look at it, "But I" is a dead end. "But God" is the only way to achieve salvation, to move from death to life, and to experience all the goodness of the Godhead.

As you honestly assess your heart and attitudes, what posture are you embracing today – "But God" or "But I"? How would the Lord like to pour out his mercy and grace on you today?

Reflection:

How do you respond to this simple and yet profound phrase – "But God"?

You Are His Workmanship
Saturday

"For by grace you have been saved through faith. And this is not your own doing, it is the gift of God, not a result of works, so that no one may boast. For we are his workmanship, created in Christ Jesus for good works, which God has prepared beforehand, that we should walk in them." Ephesians 2:8-10

Everything you have and everything you are is a gift from God – your family, your intellect, your money, your work, your personality, etc. As Psalm 139 says, *"For you formed my inward parts; you knitted me together in my mother's womb. I praise you, for I am fearfully and wonderfully made"* (Psalm 139:13-14).

You are God's idea, and you are the work of his hands. Everything about you is designed by the perfect Creator.

Not only are you designed by this perfect Creator, but you are redeemed by him. Though you are created in the image of God, you were also born into the fallen nature of sin. That is the bad news. The good news is that you have been saved from that fallen nature. Paul reiterates all throughout his letter that you are saved by the grace of God, not saved by anything you have done or will do. Salvation from sin comes from God alone.

What humbling words those are for people who like to earn and achieve! Paul goes on to say that this salvation is a gift from God so that no one can boast. This is humbling but also liberating. There are no expectations of us making our own way to God or being just good enough that he would love us. Instead, his salvation and his love are a gift. Gifts are undeserved, and they must be received with gratitude.

That gratitude propels us to live faithfully with the Lord and for the Lord. When God designed us, he had a specific plan just for us. Every aspect of our being fits together to lead us into that plan or calling for our lives. As we fulfill these good works, we bring glory to God. People see him as we lead, work, serve, and love others. In these words, Paul reminds us that we are his workmanship. The New Living Translation of these verses say that we are his masterpiece.

God delights in his workmanship, his masterpiece. He loves what he has made us to be, and he longs for us to fully embrace what he has made us to do. There is no cookie-cutter calling. Some are called to serve him as executives of companies; some are called to serve him as missionaries overseas. Some are called to teach our children in secular schools; some are called to serve as Christian Education Directors in churches. Every child of God has a calling, and every calling is just as important to the building and well-being of the kingdom of God.

Are you living in the fullness of God's grace? Are you receiving all that he has for you, and are you doing all that he has called you to do? No matter how you answer those questions, you are his workmanship. He longs to see you live fully into your calling for he knows that in fulfilling that calling, you will be blessed and you will be a blessing!

Reflection:

Spend some time today reflecting on what it means for you to be God's workmanship or masterpiece. What does he want you to know, to receive, and to do?

Week of the Fifth Sunday in Lent

The Hope to Come
Sunday

"Behold, the days are coming, declares the Lord, when I will make a new covenant with the house of Israel and the house of Judah, not like the covenant that I made with their fathers on the day when I took them by the hand to bring them out of the land of Egypt, my covenant that they broke, though I was their husband, declares the Lord. For this is the covenant that I will make with the house of Israel after those days, declares the Lord: I will put my law within them, and I will write it on their hearts. And I will be their God, and they shall be my people. And no longer shall each one teach his neighbor and each his brother, saying, 'Know the Lord,' for they shall all know me, from the least of them to the greatest, declares the Lord. For I will forgive their iniquity, and I will remember their sin no more." Jeremiah 31:31-34

Through the prophet Jeremiah, the Lord spoke hope into the nation of Israel. During Jeremiah's ministry, the nation of Israel was in exile – physically and spiritually. They had been defeated and driven from the promised land. Their defeat was the direct result of their unfaithfulness to the covenant with the Lord. Though the Lord was continually faithful to the nation of Israel, they repeatedly sinned against God; they worshipped idols, made alliances with the other nations, and did not honor or worship the Lord. The Lord repeatedly warned his people of upcoming judgment for their hard-heartedness and ongoing sin. Instead of repenting and returning to the Lord, Israel seemed intent upon its evil ways.

Sin had defeated God's people. They were in bondage to their wicked ways and rebellion against God. This defeat led to another defeat – a physical defeat. King Nebuchadnezzar of Babylon attacked and decimated the city of Jerusalem, destroyed the temple, and took many captives. The nation of Israel quickly found itself to be a people in exile.

Where was their God? The God of the Hebrews was in the place he had always been – sitting on the throne in his everlasting kingdom. He had not forgotten his people but handed them over to the consequences of their sin and rebellion. In his mercy and steadfast love, God then spoke through Jeremiah of a new hope for his people. It was the hope of restoration and a new relationship with himself.

Once again, there was hope for God's people. Unlike the nation of Israel, God was faithful to his covenantal promises to Abraham, Isaac, and Jacob. He had not forgotten, nor had he turned away. Instead, God spoke of a new covenant, a covenant of grace and inward knowing of the Lord. They were to look beyond their exile to God's future promise. In that promise, they could find hope and strength for the day.

As we enter the fifth week of Lent, the Lord invites us to look beyond today and to look forward to the celebration of Easter. On that day, we will celebrate the resurrection of Jesus, and his defeat of sin, death, and Satan. All the temptations we endure, all the setbacks we face, and all the conviction of sin will also come to an end. Like Jesus, we too, have overcome sin, death, and Satan. For now, we are like the exiles in Babylon as we live in the now but not yet. The promises of the Lord are true and trustworthy. We can live in them today, but the fulfillment will come with Jesus' return.

Reflection:

Are you living with this Easter hope? How would the Lord like to remind you of your triumph over sin, death, and Satan today?

The Power to Obey
Monday

"For this is the covenant that I will make with the house of Israel after those days, declares the Lord: I will put my law within them, and I will write it on their hearts. And I will be their God, and they shall be my people. And no longer shall each one teach his neighbor and each his brother, saying, 'Know the Lord,' for they shall all know me, from the least of them to the greatest, declares the Lord. For I will forgive their iniquity, and I will remember their sin no more." Jeremiah 31:33-34

When the Lord led his people out of the land of Egypt, he then established the Mosaic covenant with them. They were given the Ten Commandments on a tablet made of stone. Adherence and obedience to this law would set the nation of Israel apart from every other nation in the world. They would be recognized as God's chosen people, his firstborn son.

Sadly, adherence to this law proved to be quite challenging for the nation of Israel. As Moses was up on the mountain receiving the law, the Israelites were forming and then worshipping the golden calf. They were instructed to worship the Lord God alone and to make no idols for themselves. The first two commandments were broken before they even saw the tablet. Even within the promised land, God's people were constantly falling away from covenantal faithfulness and true worship of the Lord.

In his mercy and steadfast love, the Lord spoke to the exiled nation of Israel of a new covenant. Where the Mosaic covenant was purely external, this new covenant would move from the external to the internal. God would write his law on their hearts. What a powerful image! The Israelites would move from just knowing God and his law in their heads to knowing God in their hearts. Head knowledge is a good and useful thing; however, it is often when head knowledge also becomes heart knowledge that true transformation occurs.

God longed to transform his people. He longed for them to know him with all of their heart, soul, mind, and strength. In knowing their frailty, the Lord knew that an inward experience of his love, power, and presence would be necessary to lead his people into that intimate relationship with him. Where the people had long been dependent upon the priests and the prophets to teach them the ways of God, they would now be taught by God himself. They would have access to his Word, truth, and presence in a new and tangible way.

It is hard to fathom how the Israelites would receive this prophetic word from Jeremiah. Surely, many of them wanted to love and obey the Lord. They would likely have desired to understand his ways so they could better trust him. Sin hardens God's people making it difficult to whole-heartedly live for the Lord. As we read yesterday, sin is a spiritual bondage that prevents people from seeing God, from hearing God, and from obeying God.

The Lord knew and understood that bondage to sin and all the consequences of that bondage. That is why he sent his Son into the world. With the death and resurrection of Jesus Christ, the bondage to sin is broken. When one looks to Jesus and his work on the cross, he or she receives the gift of the Holy Spirit. That Holy Spirit is the very one that sets the prisoner free, opens ears and eyes, and leads a person into God's perfect will.

We are the full recipients of this prophetic word from Jeremiah. God has written his Word on our hearts; God has made us his children; God has given us understanding of himself, his truth, and his ways; God has forgiven our sins. Are we choosing to receive all that he gives and to allow the Holy Spirit full access to our lives? Are we choosing God's ways and turning from the sinful patterns that once held us?

The Holy Spirit would lead us into truth, life, and healing. May we surrender to his power today!

Reflection:

Do you recognize God's presence and power that dwells within you? How could you surrender more to the Holy Spirit today?

We Wish to See Jesus
Tuesday

"Now among those who went up to worship at the feast were some Greeks. So these came to Phillip, who was from Bethsaida in Galilee, and asked him, 'Sir, we wish to see Jesus.' Phillip went and told Andrew; Andrew and Phillip went and told Jesus." John 12:20-22

To better understand these verses of Scripture, it is helpful to look back to the preceding verse: *"Look, the world has gone after him"* (John 12:19). The Pharisees were quite concerned with the popularity of Jesus. Not only had Jesus performed many miracles among the people, but he had also raised Lazarus from the dead. Never had a Pharisee raised someone from the dead! These men were threatened as they saw the influence of Jesus increase while their influence continued to decrease.

As teachers of the law of God, these Pharisees were invited to be part of Jesus' ministry and to enjoy the fulfillment of God's promises to them and the nation of Israel. Instead of receiving and rejoicing in the Son of God, these stubborn men sought to refute him and undermine his ministry, so much so that they were planning how to kill Lazarus and destroy the evidence of his resurrection.

Despite this ongoing sabotage of the Pharisees, Jesus did continue to draw people to himself. The fact that Greeks came to the disciples of Jesus demonstrated the validity of the Pharisees' concern. Not only do these Greeks come to the disciples, but they come with a simply yet profound request: *"Sir, we wish to see Jesus"* (John 12:21). In the Gospel of John, seeing and hearing Jesus was the means of coming to faith in Jesus. In seeing and hearing, the people could understand who Jesus was – the perfect Son of God who had come into the world so that they could know the Father, the Son, and the Holy Spirit.

As we engage in this season of Lent, are we asking to see Jesus? Are we imploring the Lord to open our eyes, ears, and hearts to fully receive and understand him? Are we open to further revelation of who he is, how he has called us to live, and to seeing ourselves in his light?

When we see and hear Jesus through the power of the Holy Spirit, we cannot remain the same. God's Son came down to dwell among his people, to die on behalf of sin, and to be raised unto life so that we may have life – eternal and abundant life.

May we seek him today and as we see him, may we be transformed into those who trust him, love him, and follow him.

Reflection:

Do you wish to see Jesus? Spend some time with the Lord today contemplating these simple and yet profound words.

God's Plan of Glorification
Wednesday

"And Jesus answered them, 'The hour has come for the Son of Man to be glorified. Truly, truly, I say to you, unless a grain of wheat falls into the earth and dies, it remains alone; but if it dies, it bears much fruit. Whoever loves his life loses it, and whoever hates his life in this world will keep it for eternal life. If anyone serves me, he must follow me; and where I am, there will my servant be also. If anyone serves me, the Father will honor him.'" John 12:23-26

At this point in the text, the Greeks are seeking Jesus. In fact, they have requested to see Jesus. When that request is presented to Jesus, he provides a surprising response: *"The hour has come for the Son of Man to be glorified"* (verse 23). John's Gospel is shifting directions. Three times in the Gospel we read that it is not the hour (John 2:4, 7:6-8, 8:20). Now, the hour has come. Jesus will speak of his impending death and speak of it frequently. Where Jesus had been quick to respond to the requests of the people, he is now focused on a bigger plan, a plan of glorification.

When people thought of being glorified, the cross would be the last place they would expect that to happen. The cross was about shame and humiliation. Jesus frequently spoke of the time when he would be lifted up; of course, we know that means lifted up on the cross. For the disciples of Jesus, this term held great ambiguity.

The disciples wanted Jesus to be lifted up in earthly glory so that all would see and understand him to be the king of Israel. However, Jesus was focused on a heavenly glory where Jesus will transform shame into glory and humiliation into exaltation. After his death, the earth shook, rocks split, dead were raised, and the curtain in the temple was torn in two.

The centurion who was keeping watch over Jesus declared, *"Truly this man was the Son of God"* (See Matthew 27:51-54). Never before and never again would they behold a crucifixion like that of Jesus Christ. Jesus overcame the shame of the cross to be declared the Son of God.

Jesus knew that through his death, many would receive life. Just as a grain of wheat must die to produce fruit, so must the Son of God die to produce fruit in those who would put their trust in him. The gift of the Holy Spirit within the believer creates the fruit; Jesus is the vine and from that vine comes growth, sustenance, and renewal. As Jesus taught his disciples, the Spirit would not come unless he departed this world to return to his Father (John 16:7-8).

Jesus would invite his followers to walk as he walked, to live the abundant life in this world and then eternal life in the world to come. Like Jesus, his followers must die to the ways of this world to embrace the ways of the kingdom of God. Those who accept this invitation will find that abundant and eternal life. Die to live. Let go of the kingdom of this world to embrace the kingdom of God.

As we see in the life of Jesus, the way of abundant and eternal life is not always easy; nevertheless, the rewards will be great. Those who follow Jesus will be honored by his Father, honored in this world and the world to come.

Reflection:

How do you receive these words of Jesus? Have you been willing to die to this earthly kingdom to fully pursue the kingdom of God? Is there anything the Lord would have you die to today so that you may walk more abundantly with him and through him?

Father, Glorify Your Name
Thursday

"'Now is my soul troubled. And what shall I say? "Father, save me from this hour"? But for this purpose I have come to this hour. Father, glorify your name.' Then a voice came from heaven: 'I have glorified it, and I will glorify it again.' The crowd that stood there and heard it said that it had thundered. Others said, 'An angel has spoken to him.' Jesus answered, 'This voice has come for your sake, not mine. Now is the judgment of this world; now will the ruler of this world be cast out. And I, when I am lifted up from the earth, will draw all people to myself.' He said this to show by what kind of death he was going to die."
John 12:27-33

Knowing that his time was drawing near, Jesus acknowledged that he was troubled. The way before him would not be the easy way. Yet Jesus accepted the calling on his life and surrendered fully to what was to come. As opposed to whining, complaining, or embracing fear, Jesus modelled the Christian response to hardship: *"Father, glorify your name"* (verse 28). Personally, I would have been asking for a Plan B, but Jesus didn't seek his comfort; Jesus sought God's glory.

Following this brief and pointed prayer of Jesus came a voice from heaven: *"I have glorified it, and I will glorify it again"* (verse 28). For the third time, the voice of the Father affirms the Son. The Lord spoke at the baptism of Jesus, the transfiguration, and now as Jesus prepares himself to walk the road to Gethsemane. Jesus never doubted his identity or his calling; he didn't need the Father's voice to affirm him. Jesus heard the Father's voice constantly in his times of prayer. However, those who were present were the ones who needed to hear the voice of the heavenly Father.

All throughout the ministry of Jesus, there were those who were willing and able to see and believe, and then there were those who would not receive his words of truth. This time was no different. There were those present who claimed the voice was the sound of thunder and others who said an angel spoke to Jesus. They downplayed the miracle and missed the significance of the words of God. Jesus was the glory of the Father just as the Father was the glory of Jesus. Jesus and the Father were one.

Jesus took no offense at their unbelief though he spoke the hard truth that judgment was here. To reject the Son was to reject the Father. A person can belong to this world and the ruler of this world (Satan), or a person can belong to the kingdom of heaven and to the Lord. There were two clear options – the world/Satan or the kingdom of heaven/God. Jesus allowed the people to wrestle with this judgment and their allegiance.

As for Jesus, he was set on the will of his Father. The way ahead was certain, and that way was the cross. Jesus knew that in being lifted up on the cross, the barriers between God and people would be broken. The blood of Jesus made the way for all to become children of God. In fact, the kingdom of God expanded from focusing on the nation of Israel to all nations and all people. All were invited to look upon the crucified Savior and to find life through his atoning death.

Reflection:

Are you willing to pray the prayer of Jesus: "Father, glorify your name" in your life, in your challenges, and in your good times?

Forgiven, Cleansed, and Redeemed
Friday

"Purge me with hyssop, and I shall be clean; wash me, and I shall be whiter than snow. Let me hear joy and gladness; let the bones that you have broken rejoice. Hide your face from my sins, and blot out all my iniquities. Create in me a clean heart, O God, and renew a right spirit within me." Psalm 51:7-10

As King David penned this psalm, he was experiencing the pain of his royal failure. Not only had David sinned greatly, but he had been caught in his sin. What David tried to hide behind his royal robes and palace, God revealed through the prophet Nathan. As we see in the words of Psalm 51, David was a broken and contrite man. He saw how far he had fallen short of the glory of God and the position entrusted to him as king of Israel. Throughout Psalm 51, David fully acknowledged his sin before the Lord. He grieved for that sin and longed to be brought into a right relationship with the Lord.

King David knew he could not cleanse himself of that sin nor restore his relationship with the Lord. So, David looked to the only one who could cleanse and restore him. David asked the Lord to purge him and to wash him. David wanted every ounce of his sin to be removed from him, from his internal self and from his external self. David entrusted himself to the mercy and steadfast love of the Lord. He believed that God was not only able to cleanse and heal David but willing to cleanse and heal David.

Not only did David want to be fully cleansed, but he longed to be redeemed. He asked the Lord to restore his joy and gladness. The desire of David's heart was that God would meet him in that place of failure and sin, administer the fullness of his grace, then lead David to a new place with him, a place of joy and gladness but also of rejoicing after the pain. Redemption was not just being out of pain but seeing God work in the pain and through the pain.

King David wanted to be a man after God's own heart. To do so, he would need the Lord to turn away from his sin and shame and to create a new heart within him, a clean and pure heart. Again, David could never do this for himself. While he was one of the most powerful men of his time, King David was a man completely dependent upon the grace and love of the Lord. David could not cleanse himself of sin, could not remove the stain of that sin, could not redeem the sin and the consequences of that sin, and could not restore himself. King David looked to the Lord in full humility and with trust in God's gracious nature.

All throughout the Lenten season, we are invited to make David's prayer in this psalm our prayer. We are invited to be exposed by the light of Jesus Christ. We are invited to see our sins and shortcomings, to see all our failures to love the Lord and to walk faithfully with him. We are invited to see these things so that we can then do as David did – look to the Lord for forgiveness, for cleansing, and for redemption. Just as God longed to be merciful and gracious towards King David, so he longs to be merciful and gracious to you.

Reflection:

Are you receiving this invitation to be exposed so that you can be forgiven, cleansed, and redeemed?

Create in Me a Clean Heart
Saturday

"Create in me a clean heart, O God, and renew a right spirit within me. Cast me not away from your presence, and take not your Holy Spirit from me. Restore to me the joy of your salvation, and uphold me with a willing spirit." Psalm 51:10-11

Yesterday, we considered David's royal failure before God and his people. Today, we will consider the blessings of God's mercy and grace. David asked God to create a clean heart within him, a heart free from the lust and all the lies that resulted from that lust. He didn't stop there. David would go on to ask the Lord to renew a right spirit within him. David wanted to love the Lord and to love the Lord's people.

David wanted to live in obedience to God; he wanted to love the things that God loved and to do the things that would honor and glorify God. Yet, David also understood that he could not produce those things within himself. He needed the presence and work of the Lord. Only the Lord could renew a right spirit within a man.

Renewal of the spirit is another invitation of Lent. We can acknowledge that we don't always love God as we could; we don't love God's people; we don't follow him whole-heartedly; and we repeatedly miss the mark of holiness. God understands our inability to meet the mark and he sees our grief. In his mercy and grace, the Lord is so quick to come and to light the fire within us once again. It is the fire of his Holy Spirit.

Remember when John the Baptist foretold of the baptism of Jesus: *"I baptize you with water for repentance, but he who is coming after me is mightier than I, whose sandals I am not worthy to carry. He will baptize you with the Holy Spirit and fire"* (Matthew 3:11). The Lord longs to stoke that fire within us. That fire of the Holy Spirit is sanctifying, cleansing, healing, and renewing. With God's fire burning, we find the old ways of the flesh fading away and the new life of the Spirit flourishing within us.

When God's Holy Spirit is present and burning in our lives, we know the presence of God as we also experience the joy of our life in him. Salvation is about life, eternal life with the Father and abundant life through the Holy Spirit in this world. Even when we sin or douse the flames of that Spirit, he is there to sustain us and uphold us. The Father will not let us go though he will allow us to miss the great work of the Holy Spirit.

To keep the flame burning within us, we must be people of the light. We must be willing to see our sin, confess it to the Lord, and then to allow his mercy and grace to wash us and restore us. Our spirits are renewed as God's presence is manifested in us and through us, and we know the joy of our salvation.

Reflection:

How is your fire? How would the Lord like to cleanse your heart and renew your spirit today?

Holy Week

The Mindset of Christ
Palm Sunday

"Have this mind among yourselves, which is yours in Christ Jesus, who, though he was in the form of God, did not count equality with God a thing to be grasped, but emptied himself, by taking the form of a servant, being born in the likeness of men." Philippians 2:5-7

Paul writes challenging words here in his letter to the Philippians. These are words that we might want to leave with those in the church of Philippi; however, they are words for us today just as much as then. We, too, are instructed to have the mind of Christ. To illustrate what this mind of Christ looks like, Paul went on to write of the humility of Christ. Jesus was God, yet he gave up all his rights, privileges, and comforts to leave the heavenly realm and come dwell as one of us. Not only did Jesus come to earth as a human, but Jesus was not born in a palace as a king. Instead, Jesus was born in a stable. A stable filled with animals – their sounds, smells, and excretions. Though our modern pictures of the stable usually look quite clean and tidy, the birth experience of Jesus was a humble place, a messy place designed for animals and not the Son of God.

Paul will challenge his readers to consider that if Jesus was truly God and humbled himself to become a baby born in a stable, why are we so reluctant to embrace humility? The mindset of Jesus was exemplified in his willingness to come, to dwell among us, and to model a life of perfect submission and obedience to the Father. Jesus never demanded to be recognized as the Son of God. Jesus never demanded to be respected or admired. Instead, Jesus demonstrated the love, power, and holiness of God in all that he did without expectation for acknowledgement or glory.

The mindset of Jesus was humility, submission to the Father's will, and perfect obedience. Paul exhorts his readers to have this same mindset. In his exhortation to develop the mindset of Christ, Paul knows that it is impossible for a person to cultivate this in his or her life. What Paul writes is that this mindset is already ours in Christ Jesus. Faith in Christ allows one to live the life of Christ. When a child of God seeks to have his or her mind transformed to be like Jesus, the Holy Spirit is there willing and able to work that transformation. It may not be a comfortable process. Jesus' incarnation was surely not a comfortable process; however, it is through his pain that we receive all the rights and privileges of being a child of God.

As we come into Holy Week, take some time to ask the Lord if there is transformative work that he would like to do in you. How could you better have the mind of Christ in you? What does it look like for you to embrace this kind of humility, a humility that is willing to empty yourself and take the form of a servant in the kingdom of God? Are you truly submitting to the Father and living in obedience to his will for your life? The road to the cross requires sacrifice, yet it is the road to salvation, resurrection, and eternal life.

Reflection:

What does the Lord want to work into your mindset today? Will you surrender and obey?

Humiliation to Exaltation
Monday

"And being found in human form, he humbled himself by becoming obedient to the point of death, even death on a cross. Therefore God has highly exalted him and bestowed on him the name that is above every name, so that at the name of Jesus every knee should bow, in heaven and on earth and under the earth, and every tongue confess that Jesus Christ is Lord, to the glory of God the Father." Philippians 2:8-11

In verses five through seven of this chapter in Philippians, Paul challenged his readers to have the mind of Christ. The mind of Christ was then shown to be that of humility, submission, and obedience. Jesus modelled all these as he relinquished the glory of being one with the Father as well as all the comfort and joy of the heavenly realm. Here, Paul goes on to describe this humility of Jesus Christ. Not only did he give up this glory and comfort to become a man and dwell among us, but he was so committed to the will of his Father that he was willing to submit himself to death on a cross – the greatest experience of physical agony and shame.

Thankfully, the story of Jesus does not end at the cross. Easter is on the horizon. After Jesus' rejection, pain, and humiliation on the cross came his exaltation. After the resurrection of Jesus came the ascension of Jesus. All that Jesus left behind in the heavenly realms was restored to him. He is now one with the Father again and sits in glory above all things.

His humiliation also brought our exaltation. As the children of God, we have been lifted from death to life, from condemnation to forgiveness. We have eternal life with the triune God as our promise. To see Jesus in all his glory is our great hope and goal. Our knees bow to him here on earth and will bow to him when we get into his eternal kingdom.

What Paul wants his readers to know is that not only will our knees bow to Jesus, but every knee will bow to Jesus. Those who rejected him, those who nailed him to the cross, those who spit in the face of Jesus, those who renounce the work of the cross – EVERY knee will bow, and every tongue will confess, "Jesus Christ is Lord".

The thirty-three years that Jesus spent on earth was a time of ultimate humility, submission, and obedience. Many people did not recognize Jesus as the incarnate God, the promised Messiah. However, Jesus is now glorified by his Father. There will come a day when Jesus returns and will be glorified by all people. As his disciples, we are called to follow this example of Jesus.

We are now the ones who are called to humble ourselves, to submit to the Father's will, and to be obedient in all things. This commitment to Jesus may lead to our own humiliation in this world; however, we have the promises of exaltation. We will see the full glory of the Lord, and we will be transformed to the same eternal glory.

Reflection:

Are you able to see beyond your temporal call to humble yourself to the eternal hope of glory?

An Offering to Jesus
Tuesday

"And while he was at Bethany in the house of Simon the leper, as he was reclining at table, a woman came with an alabaster flask of ointment of pure nard, very costly, and she broke the flask and poured it over his head. There were some who said to themselves indignantly, 'Why was the ointment wasted like that? For this ointment could have been sold for more than three hundred denarii and given to the poor.' And they scolded her. But Jesus said, 'Leave her alone. Why do you trouble her? She has done a beautiful thing to me. For you always have the poor with you, and whenever you want, you can do good for them. But you will not always have me. She has done what she could; she has anointed my body beforehand for burial. And truly, I say to you, wherever the gospel is proclaimed in the whole world, what she has done will be told in memory of her.'" Mark 14:3-9

At this point in Mark's Gospel, Jesus has made his triumphal entry into Jerusalem. Palm branches were waved and placed on the road while Jesus was heralded, *"Hosanna! Blessed is he who comes in the name of the Lord! Blessed is the coming kingdom of our father David! Hosanna in the highest!"* (Mark 11:9-10). Jesus was glorified by the people and welcomed into the city of Jerusalem as the true king.

Not everyone was celebrating Jesus. Even though it is just two days prior to the Passover, the chief priests and scribes were not conspiring about how to best celebrate the special day; instead, they were conspiring about how to arrest Jesus without causing an uproar among the people.

Meanwhile, Jesus was at the home of Simon the leper. While he was enjoying time with his friends, an unnamed woman came to Jesus and poured ointment over his head. Those nearby were astounded at this great offering. They scolded the woman for pouring out such abundance upon the head of Jesus. Certainly, this money could be better used to feed the poor or to care for those in need. While they may have sounded righteous for a moment, Jesus would provide much needed insight and rebuke.

Indeed, this ointment was expensive; it was worth about a year's worth of wages. However, Jesus did not rebuke this woman for her wastefulness, but rather he affirmed her heart and her offering. This woman understood something these men weren't willing to acknowledge. She knew who Jesus was and she was aware of what was ahead of him. Those who rebuked her still didn't understand that Jesus was headed to the cross. His time with them was coming to an end. Their words revealed their hearts; they weren't focused on the way of the cross or the true way of Jesus.

In affirming this woman's offering, Jesus also said that her story would continue to be told with the Gospel. Sure enough, Mark was faithful to share her story. This story contrasts those who embrace the person and work of Jesus against those who remain intent upon their own agendas and miss Jesus and his journey to the cross.

Claiming to love Jesus is not enough, nor is saying the right things sufficient. Religious words and acts can make one appear to be holy or faithful. Instead, it is those who will put their faith and trust in the Messiah and in his work on the cross who are the true children of God, the holy and faithful ones of the Lord. These are the people who offer themselves unto him--their lives, gifts, time, and riches.

This woman saw Jesus. Her heart was to love him, to serve him, and to prepare him for what was ahead. What about us? Will we take this time to really see Jesus, to follow him in the agony of the cross, and then to marvel at the victory of his resurrection? Jesus is looking for those who want to love him, serve him, and build his kingdom. May we be the ones who step up and out to faithfully pour ourselves out as an offering unto him.

Reflection:

What challenges you in this narrative? What delights you? In what way can you offer yourself unto the Lord today?

The Spirit Is Willing but the Flesh Is Weak
Wednesday

"And they went to a place called Gethsemane. And he said to his disciples, 'Sit here while I pray.' And he took with him Peter and James and John, and began to be greatly distressed and troubled. And he said to them, 'My soul is very sorrowful, even to death. Remain here and watch.' And going a little farther, he fell on the ground and prayed that, if it were possible, the hour might pass from him. And he said, 'Abba, Father, all things are possible for you. Remove this cup from me. Yet not what I will, but what you will.' And he came and found them sleeping, and he said to Peter, 'Simon, are you asleep? Could you not watch one hour? Watch and pray that you may not enter into temptation. The spirit indeed is willing, but the flesh is weak.' And again he went away and prayed, saying the same words. And again he came and found them sleeping, for their eyes were very heavy, and they did not know what to answer him. And he came the third time and said to them, 'Are you still sleeping and taking your rest? It is enough; the hour has come. The Son of Man is betrayed into the hands of sinners. Rise, let us be going; see, my betrayer is at hand.'" Mark 14:32-42

Many good Christian people like to skip Holy Week and just celebrate Easter. It is understandable, especially as we read passages like this. How could the Son of God be on his face in the garden pleading with the Father to remove this cup from him? Jesus genuinely wrestled with the Father in prayer that night. He knew the physical and spiritual anguish that lay before him.

In the Garden of Gethsemane, we see his pain as well as his faithfulness. In his pain, Jesus continued to pray to his Father as well as to submit to his Father. This was no easy submission; instead, Jesus would demonstrate the cost of obedience in following the Father's will.

In the garden, we also see the contrast between the prayer life of Jesus and the prayer life of Peter, James, and John. Jesus asked for his closest friends to remain with him, to watch for him, and to pray for him and with him. Despite the urgency of Jesus, the disciples found it impossible to keep their eyes open.

Instead of serving Jesus, these men ended up serving the desires and demands of their flesh. Jesus spoke to this failure of his disciples: *"the spirit indeed is willing, but the flesh is weak"* (verse 38). Being in human form, Jesus fully understood the desires of the flesh and the opposition between the flesh and the spirit. His words were certainly words of disappointment in these friends but were also teaching words for their coming ministries.

This text calls us to truly see the agony of our Savior. Like us, Jesus did not want to feel the physical pain of the cross nor did he want to feel the anguish of the sins of the world coming upon him. Despite his fleshly desire to escape the cross, Jesus remained steadfast in his submission and obedience to the Father. His perfect example challenges us to consider when we are called to submit and obey.

It is unlikely that we will be called to die on a cross and impossible that we could take the sins of the world upon us. Instead, we are called to live set-apart lives for Christ. Sometimes that means choosing a career that is not heralded by the world, not engaging in a lifestyle of comfort or pleasure, not being intent on fulfilling our plans and purposes.

While we want to turn away from this harsh reality of Jesus, the Holy Spirit calls us to hear, to feel, and to align our lives with the Lord. We find that alignment in the same way Jesus did: prayer, submission, and obedience. Through this alignment with the Lord, we can choose a different way than the disciples in this passage. We can choose to deny the flesh and to heed the way of the Spirit. The invitation of Lent is to do just that.

May this Holy Week be a week in which we more fully commit ourselves to prayer, submission, and obedience to the Father.

Reflection:

How do you respond to this pain of Jesus in the garden? Do you recognize that he endured all this pain for you, out of love and a desire to have an eternal relationship with you?

Peter's Great Failure and God's Amazing Grace
Maundy Thursday

"And as Peter was below in the courtyard, one of the servant girls of the high priest came, and seeing Peter warming himself, she looked at him and said, 'You also were with the Nazarene, Jesus.' But he denied it, saying, 'I neither know nor understand what you mean.' And he went out into the gateway and the rooster crowed. And the servant girl saw him and began again to say to the bystanders, 'This man is one of them.' But again he denied it. And after a little while the bystanders again said to Peter, 'Certainly you are one of them, for you are a Galilean.' But he began to invoke a curse on himself and to swear, 'I do not know this man of whom you speak.' And immediately the rooster crowed a second time. And Peter remembered how Jesus had said to him, 'Before the rooster crows twice, you will deny me three times.' And he broke down and wept." Mark 14:66-72

We all love and understand Peter! When Jesus told the disciples that they would all betray him, Peter was quick to tell Jesus that he would not fall away. In fact, Peter claimed that even if he had to die with Jesus, he would not deny him or fall away from him (Mark 14:27-31). Peter is zealous and confident in his love and devotion to Jesus, but Peter does not comprehend what is to come and how his faith will be tested.

Despite all the times Jesus has told the disciples of his betrayal, crucifixion, and resurrection, they don't understand; they don't want to understand. They want Jesus to prove himself as the promised Messiah and to build his kingdom on earth, not in heaven. They want to keep Jesus among them, for him to keep teaching them and guiding them as he has done for the past three years. I am sure it was unfathomable to think of their Messiah, their teacher, and their friend dying on the cross. How could the only perfect man and the Son of God be put to death through the most shameful and humiliating method imaginable?

Jesus knew the tests that were to come for Peter and for all the disciples. He had warned them, and he laid a foundation upon which they would come to understand and then to build. For now, they were in the trenches with Jesus. Would they stay or would they run? Peter chose the latter.

A servant girl and bystanders questioned Peter until he had indeed denied Jesus three times, exactly as Jesus had foretold. Upon hearing the rooster crow for the second time, Peter remembered the words of Jesus, and he saw himself for who he was – a broken man in need of a Savior. With all his zeal and confidence, Peter would deny the Lord in his hour of great need.

The example of Peter is there to challenge us and to encourage us. Most of us can relate to his zeal and passion for the Lord. We, too, want to follow Jesus wholeheartedly. We feel confident that we can sustain faith through life's challenges; that we will walk with the Lord obediently for all of our days. And then we face our own times of questioning, places where our faith gets challenged.

All of us have had times when our faith was tested, or we certainly will have times when our faith will be tested. At times we will fail like Peter, but through the empowerment of the Holy Spirit, there can be even more times when we stand firm in our commitment to the Lord.

The Lord would call us to break down and weep in our times of failure but then to get right back up and start again. The grace of God covers us in our failures and then encourages us to learn, to grow, and to make new decisions that honor Christ.

Reflection:

What do you learn from this experience of Peter, and how can you apply that lesson to your own life and faith?

A Desperate Plea
Good Friday

"Be gracious to me, O Lord, for I am in distress; my eye is wasted from grief; my soul and my body also. For my life is spent with sorrow, and my years with sighing; my strength fails because of my iniquity, and my bones waste away. Because of all my adversaries I have become a reproach, especially to my neighbors, and an object of dread to my acquaintances; those who see me in the street flee from me. I have been forgotten like one who is dead; I have become like a broken vessel. For I hear the whispering of many – terror on every side! – as they scheme together against me, as they plot to take my life." Psalm 31:9-13

Some people mistakenly believe that they must get their lives cleaned up before they come to God. They offer excuses about what they need to do first – fix their marriage, break free from addiction, or clean up their thought life. The invitation of the psalms is to see that it is in our brokenness that the Lord welcomes us; it is in the places in which we see our sin, our failure, and our helpless situations that we can also see our great need for the Lord.

Psalm 31 is a psalm of lament written by David. David was a warrior king who led the nation of Israel well. He was also a man who was anointed as king then lived many years on the run, a man who had a very broken past, a man who shed far too much blood, and a man who desperately knew he needed the Lord. David was known as "a man after God's own heart" (1 Samuel 13:14). Could there be any greater description for a person? When David wrote, he wrote authentically. He was a man of great expression.

Why do we read this psalm of David on Palm Sunday? Psalm 31 as well as Psalms 22 and 69 convey the suffering of Jesus in his betrayal, the false accusations brought against him, and his painful death on the cross.

In fact, Jesus quoted Psalm 31:5 just before he died on the cross: *"Father, into your hands I commit my spirit"* (Luke 23:46). In Psalm 31, we read David's lament, and we see into the mind and heart of Jesus' lament as well.

There is grief, physical anguish, spiritual pain, sorrow, depleted strength of body and spirit, a sense of being a reproach, and feeling useless like a broken vessel. These are painful words to read! David eloquently conveyed his painful condition. In pouring out his heart to the Lord, this psalm invites us to pour our hearts out to the Lord. He is not afraid of our brokenness. He is not disappointed by our failures. He is not surprised by our sin. As we embrace our helpless and needy situation, we are invited to embrace our Savior.

Our Savior also knew pain. In fact, he knew pain that we will never know as he took our sins upon himself. The wrath of God, which we deserve, was poured out on the holy Son of God. There would be no greater anguish than that! Jesus experienced every pain that we could face in this broken world. The Lord understands you. He understands all of your pain, shame, and brokenness. Not only does he understand, but he longs to meet you in those broken places so that he can be the one to comfort you, sustain you, and ultimately heal you.

As we gaze at the cross of Christ today, can we see his pain? Jesus endured the cross because of his love for you and his desire to see you healed and set free. That healing doesn't happen in your strength; it happens in his strength. Instead of trying to get your act together, why don't you accept the invitation to fall apart, to be broken, and to desperately need a Savior? That is the invitation of Good Friday – to fully acknowledge the pain, to fully acknowledge your need for salvation, and to receive the offering that Jesus made on your behalf.

Reflection:

Are you trying to clean up your life in your power and strength? What would it look like for you to embrace your brokenness and need, then to put your eyes on the Savior?

I Trust in You, O Lord
Holy Saturday

"But I trust in you, O Lord; I say, 'You are my God.' My times are in your hand; rescue me from the hand of my enemies and from my persecutors! Make your face shine on your servant; save me in your steadfast love!" Psalm 31:14-16

This lament of David takes a turn in verse fourteen. He cried out to the Lord. In crying out, he voiced his pain and brokenness. What change occurs that moves David from lament to trust? Have his circumstances improved, or has the pain of those circumstances been lifted? We might like to assume that is the case, but I don't think so. David laid his burdens and needs before the Lord, and he trusted the Lord with those burdens and with those needs. David was a broken man who surrendered before the Father.

David put his trust in the Lord even in the difficult times. That trust allowed David to feel God's presence and comfort. He knew that God was working on his behalf despite the fact that his circumstances had not changed.

Again, David asked for the Lord to rescue him, to save him from this time of pain and rejection. David longed to feel the light of God's presence shining upon him. The light of the Lord signified his presence and his guidance, as well as his moral purity. The Lord saw through the chaos of David's life. He knew the truth, and he would stand beside David to the very end. It was that steadfast love of the Lord which provided David the comfort and strength in his troubling times.

Yesterday was Good Friday, the day when Jesus surrendered himself to the work of evil men. Jesus was falsely accused by the religious leaders of his day; he was rejected by his people; and he was handed over to the cruelest form of physical death imaginable to mankind in his day. Jesus experienced anguish – anguish of body, mind, and spirit; he felt the separation from his Father as the sin of the world came upon him. Yet, in his final breath, Jesus fully entrusted himself to the Father: *"Father, into your hands I commit my spirit!"* (Luke 23:46). These are the same words David penned at the beginning of this Psalm.

What are we to learn from the example of David and Jesus in their suffering? We can lament, cry out to the Lord, and seek to be rescued. Ultimately, the invitation is to fully entrust ourselves into the loving hands of God. His steadfast love did not fail David, did not fail Jesus, and will not fail us. It doesn't mean that our pain will end or that our circumstances will change. What it means is that we will never walk alone. The Lord will sustain us, hold us, comfort us, and ultimately bring us to the fullness of his glory.

Will you give yourself the freedom to lament, to truly feel the depths of your pain? Then, will you bring all that lament and all that pain before the Lord. He is the one who sees you perfectly, knows you perfectly, and can perfectly provide your redemption.

Reflection:

In what way is the Lord calling you to entrust yourself to him today?

Who Will Roll Away the Stone?
Easter Day

"When the Sabbath was past, Mary Magdalene, Mary the mother of James, and Salome bought spices, so that they might go and anoint him. And very early on the first day of the week, when the sun had risen, they went to the tomb. And they were saying to one another, 'Who will roll away the stone for us from the entrance of the tomb?' And looking up, they saw that the stone had been rolled back – it was very large. And entering the tomb, they saw a young man sitting on the right side, dressed in a white robe, and they were alarmed. And he said to them, 'Do not be alarmed. You seek Jesus of Nazareth, who was crucified. He has risen; he is not here. See the place where they laid him. But go, tell his disciples and Peter that he is going before you to Galilee. There you will see him, just as he told you.' And they went out and fled from the tomb, for trembling and astonishment had seized them, and they said nothing to anyone, for they were afraid." Mark 16:1-8

On this particular Sunday morning, there must have been quite a buzz around Jerusalem. Jesus, the one who had been called King of the Jews, had been crucified. His body now lay in a tomb. The religious and political leaders felt victorious for finally ridding themselves of this man who had stirred up such commotion and disturbance to their way of life. Those who followed and believed in Jesus as the Son of God were left with questions and devastating grief.

Mary Magdalene, Mary, and Salome could not just sit in their grief, so they went to the tomb of Jesus. Because his death took place on the Sabbath, proper protocols for his burial were not followed. In their love and commitment to Jesus, these women wanted to care for the body of Jesus, to care for him in his death as Jesus had cared for these women throughout his ministry.

One major question loomed in the minds of these women – "Who will roll away the stone for us from the entrance of the tomb?" There was an obstacle to getting to Jesus. His grave was covered by a massive rock. The women knew they would be unable to move that rock in their own strength. Nevertheless, they went to Jesus in all their grief and with all their uncertainty.

Much to the surprise of the women, when they got to the tomb, the rock was no longer an issue. It had been rolled away for them so that the entrance to the tomb of Jesus was unhindered. Another great surprise was the angel sitting by the tomb. It was that angel who proclaimed the greatest news ever – "Jesus has risen; he is not here!" The grave could not hold the Son of God. The enemy could not defeat him. Jesus had overcome sin, death, and all the forces of evil through his death and resurrection.

Every obstacle to the Father was removed. Mary Magdalene, Mary, and Salome had full access to Jesus and full access to the Father. Not only did these women have access, but all people could now come to the Father through the Son. Where once there were questions of how sinful people could live in relationship to a holy God, the barrier had been broken. Just as the stone had been rolled away from the tomb so that the women could see the empty grave, so the consequences of sin and death had been overcome, moved out of the way so that God's people could come without hindrance – no guilt, no shame, no fear.

Throughout this Easter season, you are invited to marvel at all that has been done for you! Salvation has been earned on your behalf; the stone has been rolled away, and you are welcome into the presence of your God.

Reflection:

Are you living in this beautiful reality? Are you rejoicing in what has been provided to you on this glorious day? The stone has been rolled away, and you are now invited to come and see this risen Lord.

www.ingramcontent.com/pod-product-compliance
Lightning Source LLC
Chambersburg PA
CBHW030529080526
44586CB00011B/372